MW01079258

Plant-Based Air Fryer Cookbook for Beginners

150 Crispy & Healthy Recipes for Everyday Cooking. Elevate Your Vegan Lifestyle with Quick, Nutrient-packed Meals

Copyright © 2024, Angelica May. All rights reserved.

No part of this publication may be reproduced, distributed, or transmitted in any form or by any means, including photocopying, recording, or other electronic or mechanical methods, without the prior written permission of the publisher, except in the case of brief quotations embodied in critical reviews and certain other non-commercial uses permitted by copyright law.

Disclaimer: The information and recipes provided in this cookbook are intended for general informational purposes only. The author and publisher make no representations or warranties of any kind, express or implied, about the completeness, accuracy, reliability, suitability, or availability of the information and recipes contained within these pages. Any reliance you place on such information is strictly at your own risk.

The recipes are based on the author's experiences and preferences, and individual results may vary. Before attempting any of the recipes or making significant changes to your diet, it is recommended that you consult with a qualified healthcare professional or nutritionist.

The author and publisher disclaim any responsibility for any adverse effects resulting directly or indirectly from the use of the information or recipes provided in this cookbook..

Table of contents

Benefits of a Plant-Based Diet

In recent years, the popularity of plant-based diets has surged as people become increasingly conscious of their health, the environment, and animal welfare. A plant-based diet involves consuming predominantly plant-derived foods while minimizing or eliminating animal products. This shift in dietary choices has been met with widespread enthusiasm, not just from vegans and vegetarians but also from individuals seeking a healthier and more sustainable lifestyle. The benefits of a plant-based diet extend far beyond personal well-being, encompassing environmental and ethical considerations as well.

One of the primary advantages of adopting a plant-based diet is its positive impact on heart health. Numerous studies have shown that plant-based diets can reduce the risk of cardiovascular diseases. The high fiber content, coupled with the absence of saturated fats found in many animal products, helps lower cholesterol levels and maintain healthy blood pressure. A diet rich in fruits, vegetables, whole grains, and nuts contributes to improved cardiovascular function, reducing the likelihood of heart-related issues.

Plant-based diets are often associated with effective weight management and weight loss. The emphasis on nutrient-dense, low-calorie foods means individuals can enjoy satisfying meals while consuming fewer overall calories. Additionally, plant-based diets are typically higher in fiber, promoting feelings of fullness and reducing the likelihood of overeating. This can be particularly beneficial for those looking to achieve or maintain a healthy weight.

Research consistently suggests that a plant-based diet is linked to a reduced risk of various chronic diseases, including type 2 diabetes, certain cancers, and hypertension. The abundance of antioxidants, vitamins, and minerals found in plant-based foods strengthens the immune system and supports overall health, creating a natural defense against chronic conditions.

A plant-based diet is inherently rich in dietary fiber, promoting optimal digestive health. Fiber aids in maintaining regular bowel movements, preventing constipation, and fostering a healthy gut microbiome. A balanced and diverse plant-based diet encourages the growth of beneficial bacteria in the digestive tract, contributing to improved digestion and nutrient absorption.

Beyond personal health benefits, choosing a plant-based diet can have a positive impact on the environment. Animal agriculture is a significant contributor to deforestation, water pollution, and greenhouse gas emissions. By opting for plant-based alternatives, individuals can reduce their ecological footprint, conserve water, and mitigate the environmental impact associated with industrial animal farming.

For many individuals, the decision to adopt a plant-based diet is rooted in ethical considerations regarding the treatment of animals. Choosing plant-based foods helps decrease the demand for animal products, leading to reduced reliance on factory farming practices. This aligns with a growing societal awareness of animal welfare issues and supports a more compassionate approach to food consumption.

The benefits of a plant-based diet extend far beyond the confines of personal health, encompassing environmental sustainability and ethical considerations. By embracing a diet rich in fruits, vegetables, whole grains, and legumes, individuals can enhance their well-being while contributing to a healthier planet. Whether motivated by health concerns, environmental consciousness, or ethical principles, the shift toward plant-based living represents a positive step toward a more sustainable and compassionate future.

Embracing a Plant-Based Lifestyle

In a contemporary world increasingly valuing health-conscious choices and sustainable living, the plant-based lifestyle has emerged as a powerful and transformative choice. Whether driven by health considerations, environmental consciousness, or ethical beliefs, adopting a plant-based diet can be a fulfilling and rewarding journey. To guide you through this lifestyle change, we present an extensive set of tips to help you embrace a plant-based diet with confidence and ease.

Educate Yourself on Nutrition. Commence your plant-based journey by delving deep into the understanding of the nutritional requirements of your body. Immerse yourself in the knowledge of essential nutrients found in plant-based foods and how to achieve a well-balanced diet. Familiarize yourself with sources of protein, iron, calcium, vitamin B12, and omega-3 fatty acids in the vast array of plant offerings.

Gradual Transition. A gradual transition can be more sustainable and comfortable, acting as a gentle introduction to the world of plant-based eating. Begin by incorporating one or two plant-based meals into your week, and progressively elevate the frequency as you become more accustomed to the lifestyle. This measured approach allows for a smoother adjustment, both for your evolving taste buds and your digestive system.

Diversify Your Plate. Embark on a culinary adventure by exploring the incredible variety of plant-based foods available. From the rainbow hues of vibrant fruits and vegetables to the heartiness of whole grains, legumes, nuts, and seeds, diversifying your plate ensures a broad spectrum of nutrients and keeps your meals exciting, enticing both your palate and your senses.

Optimize Plant-Based Protein Sources. Ensure you meet your protein requirements by strategically incorporating a diverse range of plant-based protein sources. From the humble beans and lentils to the versatile tofu, tempeh, quinoa, and edamame, enrich your meals with a mosaic of proteins. Combining different protein sources throughout the day helps ensure a complete amino acid profile, supporting your body's needs.

Prioritize Whole Foods. Elevate your commitment to health by placing a premium on whole, minimally processed foods. Let whole grains, fresh fruits, vegetables, and legumes take center stage, providing not only essential vitamins, minerals, and fiber but also contributing to a sense of satiety and sustained energy throughout the day.

Mindful Nutrient Intake. While a plant-based diet is inherently rich in nutrients, adopt a proactive stance by paying careful attention to specific vitamins and minerals that may require additional consideration. Consider incorporating supplements for nutrients like vitamin B12, vitamin D, and omega-3 fatty acids, which may be less abundant in plant-based diets.

Strategic Meal Planning. Navigate your culinary journey with foresight by strategically planning your meals. Craft a diverse menu that seamlessly integrates a mix of protein sources, a vibrant array of colorful vegetables, wholesome whole grains, and nourishing healthy fats. Preparing meals in advance not only saves time but also reduces the likelihood of opting for less healthy, convenience-driven choices.

Label Reading Awareness. Develop a keen eye for label scrutiny to identify any hidden animal products or undesirable additives. Cultivate familiarity with alternative names for animal-derived ingredients, empowering yourself to make informed and conscious choices while navigating the aisles of packaged foods. Your commitment to label reading ensures your dietary choices align with your plant-based principles.

Hydration is Key. Amplify your well-being by staying adequately hydrated through intentional consumption of water-rich fruits and vegetables, invigorating herbal teas, and refreshing infused water. Proper hydration is a cornerstone of digestive health, nutrient absorption, and overall vitality, ensuring you are poised to thrive in your plant-based lifestyle.

Connect with the Plant-Based Community. Elevate your journey by forging connections with a supportive community. Engage with like-minded individuals through vibrant social media groups, attend local meetups, or participate in online forums. Sharing experiences, triumphs, and tips with others on a similar journey not only fosters a sense of community but also enriches your plant-based experience, making the transition more enjoyable and sustainable.

Adopting a plant-based lifestyle transcends a mere dietary shift; it's a holistic approach to well-being that can positively impact your health, the environment, and animal welfare. By immersing yourself in education, embracing a gradual transition, and staying mindful of your nutritional needs, you can embark on this transformative journey with confidence and experience the manifold benefits of a plant-powered life.

Air Fryer Cooking Tips

Cooking with an air fryer has become increasingly popular due to its ability to produce crispy and delicious dishes with less oil. To help you make the most of your air frying experience, here are some essential tips for success.

The significance of preheating your air fryer mirrors the practice in traditional ovens. By allowing the cooking chamber to reach the desired temperature before introducing your ingredients, you set the stage for a culinary masterpiece. This initial heating process is instrumental in promoting even cooking, a vital factor in achieving the coveted crispiness associated with air-fried delights. Patience is key—let your air fryer preheat for a few minutes before adding your ingredients, and you'll be rewarded with consistently delicious results.

Marinating ingredients before air frying is a culinary secret that goes beyond mere taste. It's a flavor infusion process that also contributes to achieving a juicy and tender texture, transforming your dishes into culinary delights. However, a word of caution: make sure to drain off excess marinade before placing items in the air fryer. This not only prevents smoking but ensures a seamless cooking experience, allowing the flavors to shine without any unwanted interruptions. Elevate your air-fried creations with this simple yet impactful step.

The temptation to cook everything at once in your air fryer is real, but it comes with potential pitfalls. Overcrowding the basket can impede proper air circulation, leading to unevenly cooked food. To ensure optimal results, resist the urge to cram everything in. Instead, cook in batches or use layers, allowing the hot air to reach all surfaces of your ingredients. This thoughtful approach guarantees that each item gets the attention it needs, resulting in uniformly cooked and perfectly crispy dishes.

Embracing the reduced use of oil is a key advantage of air frying, but a strategic touch can elevate your results. Enhance crispiness and flavor by applying a light coating of oil to your ingredients before air frying. Utilize a cooking spray or a brush to achieve a thin, even layer, striking the perfect balance between health-conscious cooking and delectable outcomes. This small addition of oil can make a big difference in achieving the desired texture and taste in your air-fried creations.

Maintaining uniform cooking is a key to success in air frying. For items like fries or chicken wings, shake or flip your ingredients halfway through the cooking time. This not only prevents sticking but ensures that every side receives its fair share of the hot air, resulting in a perfectly crispy and evenly cooked outcome. A simple shake or flip is a small but impactful action that contributes to the overall success of your air-fried delights.

Efficiency in air fryers is undeniable, but it's crucial to adapt to variations in cooking times. The model and thickness of your ingredients play a role. Regularly check for doneness and, for proteins, rely on a meat thermometer to ensure they reach the recommended internal temperatures. This proactive approach guarantees that your dishes are not only efficient but also perfectly cooked and safe to enjoy.

Temperature versatility is a key advantage of air fryers. Experiment with different temperatures to find the sweet spot for your favorite dishes. Lower temperatures work well for dehydrating and reheating, while higher temperatures are ideal for achieving that coveted crispy exterior. Tailoring the temperature to your specific culinary needs ensures optimal results and allows you to unlock the full potential of your air fryer.

Embrace the versatility of your air fryer by exploring a world of flavors through seasonings and spices. Don't hesitate to experiment—whether it's a simple salt and pepper mix or a more complex spice blend, season

your dishes to your taste preferences. The air fryer is a culinary canvas waiting for your creativity, so let your taste buds guide you in creating uniquely seasoned and delicious meals.

Maintaining your air fryer is key to its longevity and efficiency. Regular cleaning, including the basket and tray, is essential. Refer to the manufacturer's instructions for guidance on cleaning specific parts. By keeping your air fryer well-maintained, you ensure that it continues to function efficiently and consistently produces delicious meals. Make cleaning a routine part of your air frying practice for optimal performance and lasting culinary success.

Lastly, have fun with your air fryer cooking journey. Explore new recipes, tweak cooking times, and make adjustments based on your preferences. The more you use your air fryer, the better you'll become at mastering the art of air frying. With these tips in mind, you're well on your way to creating mouthwatering, crispy delights with your air fryer.

Happy cooking!

Breakfast Delights

Sunlit Spinach Breakfast Pockets

INGREDIENTS

Ingredients:

- 2 cups fresh spinach, chopped
- 1/2 cup silken tofu, crumbled
- 1/4 cup nutritional yeast
- 1 small red onion, finely diced
- 1 clove garlic, minced
- 1/2 teaspoon turmeric (for color and slight flavor)
- Salt and pepper, to taste
- 1 tablespoon olive oil (optional, for sautéing)
- 4 vegan puff pastry sheets, thawed

 Prep Time: 15 min

 Cook Time: 12 minutes

 Serves: 4

DIRECTIONS

Sauté onions and garlic in olive oil until translucent. Add spinach, cook for 2-3 minutes. Mix crumbled silken tofu, turmeric, salt, pepper, and nutritional yeast in the pan. Heat for 2 minutes. Roll out puff pastry, cut into 6x6 inch squares. Fill with spinach-tofu mixture, fold into triangles, and seal edges. Preheat air fryer to 375°F (190°C). Air fry pockets for 10 minutes until golden brown and crisp. Allow to cool slightly before serving.

NUTRITIONAL INFORMATION

Per serving: 295 calories, 9g protein, 36g carbohydrates, 13g fat, 4g fiber, 0mg cholesterol, 420mg sodium, 320mg potassium.

Avocado Toast with a Crunchy Twist

INGREDIENTS

- 4 slices whole grain bread
- 2 ripe avocados, pitted and peeled
- Juice of 1 lemon
- Salt and black pepper, to taste
- 1/2 cup cherry tomatoes, halved
- 1/4 cup red onion, finely chopped
- 2 tablespoons pumpkin seeds (pepitas)
- 1 tablespoon chia seeds

 Prep Time: 10 min

 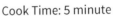 Cook Time: 5 minute

 Serves: 4

DIRECTIONS

In a bowl, mash the avocados and mix in the lemon juice, salt, and black pepper. Adjust seasoning to taste. Preheat the air fryer to 360°F (180°C). Place the bread slices in the air fryer basket in a single layer and air fry for 3 minutes or until crisp and golden brown. Spread the mashed avocado mixture evenly on the toasted bread slices. Top with cherry tomatoes, red onion, pumpkin seeds, and chia seeds. Garnish with chili flakes or herbs if desired. Serve immediately.

NUTRITIONAL INFORMATION

Per serving: 280 calories, 8g protein, 32g carbohydrates, 15g fat, 9g fiber, 0mg cholesterol, 180mg sodium, 540mg potassium.

Crispy Tofu Scramble Wraps

INGREDIENTS

- 1 block (14 oz) firm tofu, drained and crumbled
- 1 tablespoon olive oil
- 1 small yellow onion, diced
- 1 bell pepper (any color), diced
- 2 cloves garlic, minced
- 2 tablespoons nutritional yeast
- 1 teaspoon turmeric powder
- 1/2 teaspoon smoked paprika
- 1/2 teaspoon black salt (kala namak, for an "eggy" flavor) or regular salt
- Freshly ground black pepper, to taste
- 4 large vegan tortilla wraps

 Prep Time: 10 min

  Cook Time: 15 minutes

 Serves: 4

DIRECTIONS

Heat olive oil in a skillet, sauté onion, bell pepper, and garlic until tender. Add crumbled tofu, nutritional yeast, turmeric, smoked paprika, black salt, and black pepper. Cook for 5 minutes until crispy. Divide mixture onto vegan tortillas, add optional vegan cheese, salsa, and cilantro. Roll tightly, place in air fryer at 380°F for 7 minutes until crispy and golden brown.

NUTRITIONAL INFORMATION

Per serving: 330 calories, 18g protein, 38g carbohydrates, 12g fat, 4g fiber, 0mg cholesterol, 560mg sodium, 410mg potassium.

Berry Banana Air Fryer Muffins

INGREDIENTS

- 1 1/2 cups whole wheat or spelt flour
- 2 teaspoons baking powder
- 1/4 teaspoon salt
- 1/2 cup almond milk (or any other plant-based milk)
- 1/4 cup maple syrup or agave nectar
- 1 ripe banana, mashed
- 1/4 cup coconut oil, melted
- 1 teaspoon vanilla extract
- 1/2 cup mixed berries (like blueberries, raspberries, and blackberries)

 Prep Time: 15 min

 Cook Time: 12 minutes

 Serves: 6

DIRECTIONS

Whisk flour, baking powder, and salt in a large bowl. In a separate bowl, mix almond milk, maple syrup, mashed banana, melted coconut oil, and vanilla extract. Combine wet ingredients with dry, stir until just mixed. Gently fold in mixed berries. Preheat air fryer to 320°F (160°C) and place silicone muffin cups in the basket or use a muffin tin. Spoon batter into cups, filling each about 3/4 full. Air fry for 12 minutes or until toothpick comes out clean.

NUTRITIONAL INFORMATION

Per serving: 220 calories, 4g protein, 37g carbohydrates, 7g fat, 4g fiber, 0mg cholesterol, 210mg sodium, 250mg potassium.

Maple Glazed Vegan Sausage Patties

INGREDIENTS

- 1 cup textured vegetable protein (TVP)
- 1 cup boiling vegetable broth
- 1/4 cup whole wheat flour
- 2 tablespoons nutritional yeast
- 1 teaspoon garlic powder
- 1 teaspoon smoked paprika
- 1/2 teaspoon fennel seeds
- 1/2 teaspoon black pepper
- 1/4 teaspoon cayenne pepper
- 2 tablespoons soy sauce or tamari
- 3 tablespoons maple syrup

 Prep Time: 15 minutes

 Cook Time: 10 minutes

 Serves: 4

DIRECTIONS

In a bowl, pour the boiling vegetable broth over the TVP and let it sit for 10 minutes, or until the TVP is soft and has absorbed most of the liquid. Add flour, nutritional yeast, garlic powder, smoked paprika, fennel seeds, black pepper, cayenne pepper, and soy sauce to the rehydrated TVP. Mix well until combined. Divide and shape into 8 patties. Preheat the air fryer to 375°F (190°C). Brush both sides of each patty lightly with olive oil. Place the patties in a single layer in the air fryer basket. Cook for 8 minutes, flipping halfway through. In the last 2 minutes, brush the tops with maple syrup for a sweet glaze. Serve immediately with your favorite breakfast sides.

NUTRITIONAL INFORMATION

Per serving: 210 calories, 12g protein, 28g carbohydrates, 4g fat, 4g fiber, 0mg cholesterol, 530mg sodium, 320mg potassium.

Air-Fried French Toast Sticks

INGREDIENTS

- 4 slices whole grain bread
- 1/2 cup almond milk (or other plant-based milk)
- 1 tablespoon ground flaxseed
- 1 teaspoon vanilla extract
- 1/2 teaspoon ground cinnamon
- 1/4 teaspoon nutmeg
- 2 tablespoons maple syrup, plus extra for dipping
- Cooking spray or melted coconut oil for brushing

 Prep Time: 10 min

 Cook Time: 8 minutes

 Serves: 4

DIRECTIONS

In a shallow dish, whisk together almond milk, ground flaxseed, vanilla extract, cinnamon, nutmeg, and maple syrup. Let the mixture sit for 3-4 minutes to thicken slightly. Cut each bread slice into 3 or 4 sticks. Dip each stick into the almond milk mixture, ensuring all sides are coated, and let any excess drip off.

Preheat the air fryer to 370°F (188°C). Lightly brush the air fryer basket with cooking spray or melted coconut oil. Place the coated bread sticks in a single layer, ensuring they don't touch. Air fry for 8 minutes, turning halfway through, or until golden brown and crispy. Serve immediately with extra maple syrup for dipping.

NUTRITIONAL INFORMATION

Per serving: 140 calories, 5g protein, 25g carbohydrates, 3g fat, 4g fiber, 0mg cholesterol, 150mg sodium, 180mg potassium.

Crunchy Chia Seed Granola

INGREDIENTS

- 2 cups rolled oats
- 1/3 cup chia seeds
- 1/2 cup raw nuts (like almonds or walnuts), roughly chopped
- 1/4 cup dried fruit (like raisins or dried cranberries)
- 1/4 cup coconut flakes
- 1/4 cup maple syrup or agave nectar
- 2 tablespoons coconut oil, melted
- 1 teaspoon vanilla extract
- 1/2 teaspoon ground cinnamon
- A pinch of salt

Prep Time: 10 min

Cook Time: 10 minutes

Serves: 4

DIRECTIONS

In a large mixing bowl, combine rolled oats, chia seeds, nuts, dried fruit, and coconut flakes. In a separate bowl, whisk together maple syrup, melted coconut oil, vanilla extract, ground cinnamon, and salt. Pour this mixture over the oat mixture and stir until everything is well coated. Preheat the air fryer to 320°F (160°C). Spread the granola mixture in a thin layer in the air fryer basket. You may need to cook in batches depending on the size of your air fryer. Air fry for 10 minutes, stirring every 3 minutes to ensure even cooking and prevent burning. Let the granola cool completely in the air fryer basket. It will become crunchier as it cools.

NUTRITIONAL INFORMATION

Per serving: 360 calories, 10g protein, 48g carbohydrates, 16g fat, 9g fiber, 0mg cholesterol, 10mg sodium, 290mg potassium.

Morning Veggie Hash Browns

INGREDIENTS

- 2 large russet potatoes, peeled and grated
- 1 medium carrot, peeled and grated
- 1 zucchini, grated
- 1/4 cup red bell pepper, finely diced
- 1/4 cup green onion, finely chopped
- 2 tablespoons ground flaxseed mixed with 5 tablespoons water (flax egg)
- 1/4 teaspoon smoked paprika
- Salt and pepper, to taste
- 2 tablespoons olive oil or melted coconut oil

Prep Time: 15 min

Cook Time: 20 minutes

Serves: 4

DIRECTIONS

In a large mixing bowl, combine grated potatoes, carrot, zucchini, red bell pepper, and green onion. Press out as much moisture as possible using a clean kitchen towel or paper towels. Add the flax egg, smoked paprika, salt, and pepper to the bowl. Mix well until everything is well combined. Preheat the air fryer to 370°F (188°C). Form the mixture into small patties, brush both sides with olive or coconut oil, and place them in a single layer in the air fryer basket.

Air fry for 20 minutes, turning halfway through, until the hash browns are golden and crispy on the outside. Serve hot with your favorite dip or breakfast accompaniment.

NUTRITIONAL INFORMATION

Per serving: 220 calories, 5g protein, 38g carbohydrates, 7g fat, 5g fiber, 0mg cholesterol, 75mg sodium, 650mg potassium.

Cinnamon Apple Fritters

INGREDIENTS

- 1 cup all-purpose flour (or gluten-free flour blend)
- 1 1/2 teaspoons baking powder
- 2 tablespoons coconut sugar or brown sugar
- 1/2 teaspoon ground cinnamon
- A pinch of salt
- 1/2 cup almond milk (or other plant-based milk)
- 1 flax egg (1 tablespoon ground flaxseed mixed with 2.5 tablespoons water)
- 1 medium apple, peeled, cored, and diced
- 1 teaspoon vanilla extract

 Prep Time: 15 min

 Cook Time: 12 minutes

 Serves: 4

DIRECTIONS

In a mixing bowl, combine flour, baking powder, coconut sugar, cinnamon, and salt. In another bowl, prepare the flax egg by mixing ground flaxseed with water and letting it sit for a few minutes. Pour the almond milk and vanilla extract into the dry mixture, then add the flax egg. Mix until just combined. Fold in the diced apple pieces. Preheat the air fryer to 360°F (182°C). Using a spoon, drop dollops of the batter into the air fryer basket, ensuring there's enough space between each. Brush or spray the tops lightly with coconut oil. Air fry for 12 minutes, flipping halfway, until they're golden brown and cooked through. If desired, dust the fritters with powdered sugar before serving.

NUTRITIONAL INFORMATION

Per serving: 180 calories, 4g protein, 38g carbohydrates, 2g fat, 3g fiber, 0mg cholesterol, 130mg sodium, 120mg potassium.

Spiced Pumpkin Waffle Bites

INGREDIENTS

- 1 cup all-purpose flour (or gluten-free flour blend)
- 1 1/2 teaspoons baking powder
- 2 tablespoons maple syrup
- 1/4 cup pumpkin puree (not pumpkin pie filling)
- 1 teaspoon pumpkin pie spice
- A pinch of salt
- 3/4 cup almond milk (or other plant-based milk)
- 1 flax egg (1 tablespoon ground flaxseed mixed with 2.5 tablespoons water)
- 1 teaspoon vanilla extract

 Prep Time: 10 min

 Cook Time: 10 minutes

 Serves: 4 servings

DIRECTIONS

In a mixing bowl, whisk together the flour, baking powder, pumpkin pie spice, and salt. In a separate bowl, combine the pumpkin puree, almond milk, maple syrup, vanilla extract, and prepared flax egg. Pour the wet mixture into the dry ingredients and stir until just combined, taking care not to overmix. Preheat the air fryer to 375°F (190°C). Spoon the batter into a silicone waffle mold or directly onto the air fryer basket, making sure they're not too thick and there's enough space around each. Air fry for 10 minutes or until they're golden brown and cooked through, flipping halfway if not using a mold. Allow to cool slightly and then serve with additional maple syrup or toppings of choice.

NUTRITIONAL INFORMATION

Per serving: 165 calories, 4g protein, 35g carbohydrates, 2g fat, 3g fiber, 0mg cholesterol, 95mg sodium, 110mg potassium.

Zesty Tomato Breakfast Bruschetta

INGREDIENTS

- 4 slices of whole grain or sourdough bread
- 2 large ripe tomatoes, diced
- 1 small red onion, finely chopped
- 2 cloves garlic, minced
- 1 tablespoon olive oil
- 1 tablespoon balsamic vinegar
- A handful of fresh basil, chopped
- Salt and pepper to taste
- Cooking spray or additional olive oil for brushing
- Optional: nutritional yeast or vegan parmesan for sprinkling

Prep Time: 10 min

Cook Time: 5 minutes

Serves: 4

DIRECTIONS

In a bowl, combine the diced tomatoes, chopped red onion, minced garlic, olive oil, balsamic vinegar, chopped basil, salt, and pepper. Mix well and let it sit for a few minutes to allow flavors to meld. Preheat the air fryer to 350°F (175°C). Lightly brush each side of the bread slices with cooking spray or olive oil. Place the bread slices in the air fryer and cook for 3-4 minutes, flipping once until they are crispy and golden brown. Once the bread is toasted, remove it from the air fryer and top each slice generously with the tomato mixture. Sprinkle with optional nutritional yeast or vegan parmesan for added flavor. Serve immediately and enjoy!

NUTRITIONAL INFORMATION

Per serving: 140 calories, 4g protein, 24g carbohydrates, 4g fat, 3g fiber, 0mg cholesterol, 200mg sodium, 180mg potassium.

Almond Butter & Fruit Stuffed Crepes

INGREDIENTS

- 1 cup chickpea flour (gram flour)
- 1 1/2 cups almond milk (unsweetened)
- 1 tbsp ground flaxseed mixed with 2.5 tbsp water (flax egg)
- Pinch of salt
- 1 tsp vanilla extract
- 1/2 cup almond butter
- 2 bananas, thinly sliced
- 1 cup strawberries, thinly sliced
- 1 tbsp coconut oil (for brushing)

Prep Time: 20 min

Cook Time: 15 minutes

Serves: 4

DIRECTIONS

Whisk chickpea flour, almond milk, flax egg, salt, and vanilla extract in a bowl. Let the batter rest for 10 minutes. Preheat air fryer to 320°F and lightly brush the basket with coconut oil. Pour a quarter of the batter, tilt to spread thinly, and cook for 3-4 minutes. Flip and cook for 1-2 minutes. Transfer to a plate, spread almond butter, add banana and strawberry slices, fold, and repeat. Serve crepes with agave nectar or maple syrup and a dusting of powdered sugar if desired.

NUTRITIONAL INFORMATION

Per serving: 380 calories, 12g protein, 42g carbohydrates, 20g fat, 7g fiber, 0mg cholesterol, 150mg sodium, 600mg potassium.

Savory Breakfast Potato Boats

INGREDIENTS

- 4 medium russet potatoes
- 1 tbsp olive oil
- 1/2 cup diced red bell pepper
- 1/2 cup diced onion
- 1 cup chopped fresh spinach
- 1/2 cup firm tofu, crumbled
- 1 tsp turmeric powder
- Salt and pepper to taste
- 2 tbsp nutritional yeast (optional for cheesy flavor)
- Fresh chives for garnish

 Prep Time: 15 min

 Cook Time: 30 minutes

 Serves: 4

DIRECTIONS

Wash and scrub the potatoes clean. Poke several holes into each with a fork. Cook in the air fryer at 400°F (200°C) for about 20 minutes, or until fork-tender. Once cooled slightly, cut a thin slice off the top of each potato and carefully scoop out the insides, leaving a 1/4-inch wall. Reserve the scooped potato for another use or discard. In a skillet over medium heat, add olive oil, red bell pepper, and onion. Sauté until softened. Add crumbled tofu, turmeric, salt, pepper, and nutritional yeast. Stir well until combined and tofu is heated through. Finally, stir in the chopped spinach until wilted. Stuff each potato boat with the tofu mixture. Place the filled potato boats in the air fryer and cook at 370°F (185°C) for 10 minutes to reheat and slightly crisp the edges. Garnish with chopped fresh chives before serving.

NUTRITIONAL INFORMATION

Per serving: 280 calories, 8g protein, 52g carbohydrates, 4g fat, 7g fiber, 0mg cholesterol, 90mg sodium, 1100mg potassium.

Golden Turmeric Breakfast Bites

INGREDIENTS

- 1 cup chickpea flour
- 1 1/2 cups water
- 2 tbsp olive oil
- 1 tsp turmeric powder
- 1/2 tsp black pepper
- 1/2 tsp salt
- 1/4 cup finely chopped spinach
- 2 tbsp finely chopped red bell pepper
- 2 tbsp finely chopped red onion
- 1 tbsp chia seeds

 Prep Time: 10 min

 Cook Time: 15 minutes

 Serves: 4

DIRECTIONS

In a mixing bowl, combine chickpea flour, water, olive oil, turmeric powder, black pepper, and salt. Whisk until you have a smooth batter. Fold in the chopped spinach, red bell pepper, red onion, and chia seeds. Pour the mixture into silicone muffin molds or any air fryer safe mold, filling each about 3/4 full. Place the molds in the air fryer and cook at 375°F (190°C) for 15 minutes, or until a toothpick inserted into the center comes out clean. Let them cool for a couple of minutes before serving.

NUTRITIONAL INFORMATION

Per serving: 180 calories, 7g protein, 21g carbohydrates, 7g fat, 5g fiber, 0mg cholesterol, 310mg sodium, 300mg potassium.

Snack Attack

Crispy Chickpea Poppers

INGREDIENTS

- 2 cups canned chickpeas, drained and rinsed
- 1 tbsp olive oil
- 1 tsp smoked paprika
- 1/2 tsp garlic powder
- 1/2 tsp onion powder
- 1/4 tsp cayenne pepper (optional for added heat)
- Salt to taste

 Prep Time: 10 min

 Cook Time: 10 minutes

 Serves: 4

DIRECTIONS

Pat chickpeas dry with a paper towel, removing any loose skins. In a mixing bowl, combine chickpeas with olive oil, smoked paprika, garlic powder, onion powder, cayenne pepper (if using), and salt. Mix well until chickpeas are evenly coated. Place the seasoned chickpeas in a single layer in the air fryer basket. Air fry at 400°F (205°C) for 20 minutes, shaking the basket halfway through, until chickpeas are crispy and golden. Let them cool slightly before serving as they'll continue to crisp up.

NUTRITIONAL INFORMATION

Per serving: 150 calories, 7g protein, 20g carbohydrates, 5g fat, 6g fiber, 0mg cholesterol, 310mg sodium, 240mg potassium.

Zucchini Fries with Lemon Aioli

INGREDIENTS

- 2 medium zucchinis
- 1/2 cup almond flour or bread crumbs (ensure it's plant-based/vegan if using bread crumbs)
- 1 tsp dried oregano
- 1/2 tsp garlic powder
- 1/4 tsp paprika
- 1/2 cup unsweetened plant-based milk (e.g., almond milk)
- 1/2 cup vegan mayonnaise
- 1 clove garlic, minced
- Zest and juice of 1 lemon
- Salt to taste

 Prep Time: 15 minutes

 Cook Time: 12 minutes

 Serves: 4

DIRECTIONS

Cut zucchini into fries or baton shapes. Place them on paper towels and sprinkle with a bit of salt. Let them sit for 5 minutes to draw out excess moisture, then pat dry. In a shallow dish, mix almond flour (or bread crumbs), oregano, garlic powder, paprika, and salt. Pour plant-based milk into another shallow dish. Dip zucchini pieces first into milk and then coat with the almond flour mixture. Ensure they're fully coated and place them in a single layer in the air fryer basket. Air fry at 390°F (200°C) for 12 minutes or until golden and crispy, turning halfway through. For the aioli: In a small bowl, mix together vegan mayonnaise, minced garlic, lemon zest, lemon juice, and salt. Serve alongside the zucchini fries.

NUTRITIONAL INFORMATION

Per serving: 220 calories, 4g protein, 16g carbohydrates, 16g fat, 4g fiber, 0mg cholesterol, 290mg sodium, 350mg potassium.

Spicy Buffalo Cauliflower Bites

INGREDIENTS

- 1 large cauliflower head, cut into bite-sized florets
- 1/2 cup almond flour
- 1/2 cup water
- 1 tsp garlic powder
- 1/2 tsp onion powder
- 1/4 tsp salt
- 1/4 tsp black pepper
- 3/4 cup buffalo hot sauce (ensure it's vegan)
- 2 tbsp plant-based butter, melted

 Prep Time: 15 min

 Cook Time: 20 minutes

 Serves: 4

DIRECTIONS

In a large bowl, whisk together almond flour, water, garlic powder, onion powder, salt, and pepper. This will form a batter. Dip each cauliflower floret into the batter, ensuring it's fully coated, and then place in a single layer in the air fryer basket. Make sure they aren't touching to ensure even cooking. Air fry at 375°F (190°C) for 15 minutes. In a separate bowl, mix together the buffalo hot sauce and melted plant-based butter. Once the cauliflower bites are done, toss them in this spicy mixture to coat evenly. Return the coated cauliflower bites to the air fryer and cook for an additional 5 minutes or until they achieve a crispy texture.

NUTRITIONAL INFORMATION

Per serving: 110 calories, 4g protein, 8g carbohydrates, 7g fat, 3g fiber, 0mg cholesterol, 890mg sodium, 430mg potassium.

Garlic Herb Edamame

INGREDIENTS

- 2 cups frozen edamame, shelled
- 2 tbsp olive oil
- 3 garlic cloves, minced
- 1 tsp dried rosemary
- 1 tsp dried thyme
- Salt to taste
- Freshly ground black pepper to taste
- Zest of 1 lemon
- 1 tbsp lemon juice

 Prep Time: 10 min

 Cook Time: 1- minutes

Serves: 4

DIRECTIONS

In a mixing bowl, combine the olive oil, minced garlic, rosemary, thyme, lemon zest, lemon juice, salt, and pepper. Mix well to form a flavorful coating. Add in the frozen edamame and toss to coat them evenly with the herb mixture. Preheat the air fryer to 375°F (190°C). Place the edamame in a single layer in the air fryer basket. Air fry for 10 minutes, shaking the basket halfway through to ensure even cooking. Once done, transfer to a serving bowl and enjoy hot.

NUTRITIONAL INFORMATION

Per serving: 180 calories, 12g protein, 9g carbohydrates, 11g fat, 5g fiber, 0mg cholesterol, 15mg sodium, 490mg potassium.

Sweet Potato Chips with Rosemary Salt

INGREDIENTS

- 2 large sweet potatoes, thinly sliced (preferably with a mandolin)
- 1 tbsp olive oil
- 2 tsp fresh rosemary, finely chopped
- 1 tsp sea salt
- 1/4 tsp black pepper

Prep Time: 15 min

Cook Time: 20 minutes

Serves: 4

DIRECTIONS

In a large mixing bowl, toss the thinly sliced sweet potatoes with olive oil until they are well-coated. In a separate small bowl, combine the finely chopped rosemary with sea salt and black pepper. Preheat the air fryer to 350°F (175°C). Arrange the sweet potato slices in a single layer in the air fryer basket, ensuring they don't overlap. Air fry for 20 minutes or until crispy, turning the slices halfway through to ensure even cooking. Once done, transfer the chips to a serving bowl and sprinkle with the rosemary salt mixture while still hot.

NUTRITIONAL INFORMATION

Per serving: 110 calories, 2g protein, 24g carbohydrates, 3g fat, 4g fiber, 0mg cholesterol, 620mg sodium, 400mg potassium.

Air Fryer Polenta Crisps

INGREDIENTS

- 1 tube (18 oz) of pre-cooked polenta, sliced into 1/4-inch rounds
- 2 tbsp olive oil
- 1 tsp smoked paprika (or regular paprika)
- 1/2 tsp garlic powder
- Salt and pepper, to taste
- Fresh herbs (like rosemary or thyme) for garnish, optional

Prep Time: 10 min

Cook Time: 15 minutes

Serves: 4

DIRECTIONS

In a large mixing bowl, toss the polenta rounds with olive oil, paprika, garlic powder, salt, and pepper until each round is well-coated. Preheat the air fryer to 375°F (190°C). Arrange the polenta slices in a single layer in the air fryer basket, ensuring they don't overlap. Air fry for 15 minutes or until golden and crispy, turning halfway through to ensure even cooking. Once done, transfer the crisps to a serving plate and garnish with fresh herbs if desired. Serve immediately.

NUTRITIONAL INFORMATION

Per serving: 160 calories, 3g protein, 28g carbohydrates, 4g fat, 2g fiber, 0mg cholesterol, 420mg sodium, 60mg potassium.

Plantain Chips with Chili Lime Seasoning

INGREDIENTS

- 2 large green plantains, peeled and sliced into 1/8-inch thick rounds
- 2 tbsp olive oil
- 1 tsp chili powder
- Zest of 1 lime
- 1/4 tsp ground cumin
- Salt, to taste

Prep Time: 10 min   Cook Time: 16 minutes   Serves: 4

DIRECTIONS

In a large bowl, toss the plantain slices with olive oil ensuring each slice is well-coated. In a small bowl, mix chili powder, lime zest, cumin, and salt. Sprinkle this mixture over the plantain slices and toss again to coat evenly. Preheat the air fryer to 350°F (175°C). Arrange the plantain slices in a single layer in the air fryer basket, making sure they do not overlap. Air fry for 16 minutes, or until the chips are crispy and golden brown, turning them halfway through the cooking process.

NUTRITIONAL INFORMATION

Per serving: 180 calories, 1g protein, 37g carbohydrates, 7g fat, 2g fiber, 0mg cholesterol, 90mg sodium, 500mg potassium.

Crispy Kale Chips with Nutritional Yeast

INGREDIENTS

- 1 bunch of kale, washed, dried, and torn into bite-sized pieces (stems removed)
- 2 tbsp olive oil
- 2 tbsp nutritional yeast
- 1/2 tsp salt
- 1/4 tsp black pepper

Prep Time: 10 min   Cook Time: 10 minutes   Serves: 4

DIRECTIONS

In a large bowl, massage the kale with olive oil, ensuring each leaf is well-coated. Sprinkle the nutritional yeast, salt, and pepper over the kale and toss to combine. Preheat the air fryer to 300°F (150°C). Spread the kale in a single layer in the air fryer basket, ensuring no overlapping. Air fry for 10 minutes, or until the kale chips are crispy, shaking the basket or turning the kale halfway through.

NUTRITIONAL INFORMATION

Per serving: 80 calories, 3g protein, 7g carbohydrates, 5g fat, 2g fiber, 0mg cholesterol, 310mg sodium, 330mg potassium.

Lemon Pepper Brussels Sprouts

INGREDIENTS

- 1 lb Brussels sprouts, trimmed and halved
- 2 tbsp olive oil
- Zest of 1 lemon
- 2 tsp lemon juice
- 1 tsp freshly ground black pepper
- 1/2 tsp sea salt

Prep Time: 10 min

Cook Time: 15 minutes

Serves: 4

DIRECTIONS

In a large bowl, combine Brussels sprouts, olive oil, lemon zest, lemon juice, black pepper, and salt. Toss to ensure the sprouts are well-coated. Preheat the air fryer to 375°F (190°C). Arrange the Brussels sprouts in a single layer in the air fryer basket. Cook for 15 minutes, shaking the basket or turning the sprouts halfway through, until they are golden brown and crispy on the outside. Once done, transfer to a serving plate and enjoy while hot.

NUTRITIONAL INFORMATION

Per serving: 100 calories, 3g protein, 10g carbohydrates, 7g fat, 4g fiber, 0mg cholesterol, 320mg sodium, 450mg potassium.

Air-Fried Spring Rolls with Hoisin Dip

INGREDIENTS

For the Spring Rolls:

- 8 rice paper wrappers
- 1 cup thinly sliced red bell pepper
- 1 cup thinly sliced cucumber
- 1 cup shredded carrots
- 1 cup thinly sliced avocado
- 1/2 cup fresh cilantro leaves
- 1/2 cup fresh mint leaves
- 1 tbsp sesame oil

For the Hoisin Dip:

- 1/4 cup hoisin sauce
- 1 tbsp soy sauce (low sodium)
- 1 tbsp lime juice
- 1 tsp freshly grated ginger

Prep Time: 20 min

Cook Time: 10 minutes

Serves: 4

DIRECTIONS

Prepare the vegetables and herbs by washing and cutting them as indicated. Dip one rice paper wrapper into water to soften it. Lay it flat on a work surface and place a portion of each vegetable and herb towards the bottom. Roll it up tightly, tucking in the sides as you go. Brush each spring roll lightly with sesame oil. Preheat the air fryer to 370°F (190°C). Place the spring rolls in the air fryer basket, ensuring they don't touch. Cook for 10 minutes, turning once until they are golden and slightly crispy. For the dip: Mix hoisin sauce, soy sauce, lime juice, and ginger in a bowl. Serve alongside the hot spring rolls.

NUTRITIONAL INFORMATION

Per serving: 210 calories, 4g protein, 32g carbohydrates, 8g fat, 5g fiber, 0mg cholesterol, 420mg sodium, 520mg potassium.

Olive & Sundried Tomato Tapenade Tarts

INGREDIENTS

For the Tapenade:

- 1/2 cup black olives, pitted
- 1/4 cup sundried tomatoes, drained
- 2 garlic cloves
- 2 tbsp capers, drained
- 2 tbsp fresh basil leaves
- 1 tbsp olive oil
- 1 tsp lemon juice
- Salt and pepper, to taste

For the Tarts:

- 4 vegan puff pastry squares (store-bought or homemade)
- Fresh basil, for garnish

Prep Time: 15 min   Cook Time: 8 minutes   Serves: 4

DIRECTIONS

In a food processor, combine olives, sundried tomatoes, garlic, capers, basil, olive oil, lemon juice, salt, and pepper. Blend until a paste forms, scraping down the sides as necessary. Set aside. Roll out the puff pastry squares slightly to thin them out. Using a fork, prick the surface to prevent excessive puffing during cooking. Spread a generous amount of tapenade over each puff pastry square, leaving a small border around the edges. Preheat the air fryer to 350°F (175°C). Place the tarts in the air fryer basket without overlapping. Cook for 8 minutes or until the edges are golden brown and crisp. Remove from the air fryer, garnish with fresh basil, and serve warm.

NUTRITIONAL INFORMATION

Per serving: 290 calories, 5g protein, 28g carbohydrates, 18g fat, 2g fiber, 0mg cholesterol, 420mg sodium, 300mg potassium.

Spinach & Artichoke Dip Stuffed Mushrooms

INGREDIENTS

- 12 large white button mushrooms, stems removed and finely chopped (reserve caps for stuffing)
- 1 cup fresh spinach, finely chopped
- 1/2 cup artichoke hearts, drained and finely chopped
- 1/4 cup vegan cream cheese
- 2 tbsp nutritional yeast
- 2 garlic cloves, minced
- 1 tbsp olive oil
- Salt and pepper, to taste
- Fresh parsley, for garnish (optional)

Prep Time: 20 min   Cook Time: 10 minutes   Serves: 4

DIRECTIONS

In a bowl, mix together chopped mushroom stems, spinach, artichoke hearts, vegan cream cheese, nutritional yeast, and minced garlic. Season with salt and pepper, and mix until well combined. Carefully stuff each mushroom cap with the spinach and artichoke mixture, pressing down gently to pack the filling.

Lightly brush the outside of each stuffed mushroom with olive oil. Preheat the air fryer to 360°F (182°C). Place the stuffed mushrooms in the air fryer basket in a single layer, ensuring they don't touch. Cook for 10 minutes, or until mushrooms are tender and the filling is slightly golden. Remove from the air fryer, garnish with fresh parsley if desired, and serve warm.

NUTRITIONAL INFORMATION

Per serving: 120 calories, 5g protein, 8g carbohydrates, 7g fat, 3g fiber, 0mg cholesterol, 190mg sodium, 420mg potassium.

Vegan Mozzarella Sticks

INGREDIENTS

- 1 cup vegan mozzarella cheese, cut into sticks
- 1/2 cup almond milk (or any plant-based milk)
- 1 tsp apple cider vinegar
- 1 cup bread crumbs (ensure vegan-friendly)
- 1 tsp dried oregano
- 1 tsp dried basil
- 1/2 tsp garlic powder
- 1/4 tsp salt
- 1/4 tsp black pepper
- Cooking spray or olive oil for light brushing

 Prep Time: 15 minutes

 Cook Time: 10 minutes

 Serves: 4

DIRECTIONS

In a bowl, combine the almond milk and apple cider vinegar. Let it sit for a couple of minutes to curdle. In a separate bowl, mix bread crumbs, oregano, basil, garlic powder, salt, and pepper. Dip each vegan mozzarella stick into the almond milk mixture, ensuring it's well coated. Then roll it in the bread crumb mixture, pressing gently to adhere. Place the coated mozzarella sticks on a tray and freeze for at least 2 hours, or until firm. Preheat the air fryer to 370°F (188°C). Lightly brush or spray the mozzarella sticks with oil. Arrange them in a single layer in the air fryer basket, ensuring they don't touch. Cook for 10 minutes, turning halfway, or until golden and crispy.

NUTRITIONAL INFORMATION

Per serving: 220 calories, 6g protein, 30g carbohydrates, 8g fat, 3g fiber, 0mg cholesterol, 480mg sodium, 150mg potassium.

Crispy Vegan "Chicken" Nuggets

INGREDIENTS

- 1 cup vital wheat gluten
- 1/2 cup vegetable broth
- 2 tbsp nutritional yeast
- 1 tsp onion powder
- 1 tsp garlic powder
- 1/2 tsp black pepper
- 1 cup bread crumbs (ensure vegan-friendly)
- 1/2 cup unsweetened almond milk (or any plant-based milk)
- 1 tbsp ground flaxseed
- Cooking spray or olive oil for light brushing

 Prep Time: 15 min

 Cook Time: 12 minutes

 Serves: 4

DIRECTIONS

In a bowl, mix the vital wheat gluten, nutritional yeast, onion powder, garlic powder, black pepper, and vegetable broth until a dough forms. Knead for 2-3 minutes until elastic. Tear or cut the dough into small nugget-sized pieces. In a separate bowl, combine the almond milk and ground flaxseed. In another bowl, have the bread crumbs ready. Dip each nugget piece into the almond milk mixture. Then roll it in the bread crumbs, pressing gently to adhere. Preheat the air fryer to 375°F (190°C). Lightly brush or spray the nuggets with oil. Arrange them in a single layer in the air fryer basket, ensuring they don't touch. Cook for 12 minutes, turning halfway, or until golden and crispy.

NUTRITIONAL INFORMATION

Per serving: 220 calories, 15g protein, 25g carbohydrates, 6g fat, 3g fiber, 0mg cholesterol, 350mg sodium, 180mg potassium.

Leafy Greens & Things

Garlic Lemon Asparagus Spears

INGREDIENTS

- 1 lb fresh asparagus spears, trimmed
- 2 tbsp olive oil
- 3 garlic cloves, minced
- Zest and juice of 1 lemon
- Salt and pepper, to taste

Prep Time: 10 min

Cook Time: 8 minutes

Serves: 4

DIRECTIONS

In a mixing bowl, toss asparagus spears with olive oil, minced garlic, lemon zest, and lemon juice until well-coated. Preheat the air fryer to 375°F (190°C). Arrange the asparagus spears in the air fryer basket in a single layer. Cook in the air fryer for 6-8 minutes or until tender and slightly crispy, shaking the basket halfway through. Season with salt and pepper to taste, and serve immediately.

NUTRITIONAL INFORMATION

Per serving: 90 calories, 2.5g protein, 7g carbohydrates, 7g fat, 3g fiber, 0mg cholesterol, 2mg sodium, 230mg potassium.

Brussels Sprout & Pecan Toss

INGREDIENTS

- 1 lb Brussels sprouts, trimmed and halved
- 1 cup pecan halves
- 2 tbsp olive oil
- Salt and pepper, to taste
- 1 tsp maple syrup
- Zest of 1 lemon

Prep Time: 15 min

Cook Time: 12 minutes

Serves: 4

DIRECTIONS

In a mixing bowl, toss Brussels sprouts with olive oil, ensuring they are well-coated. Preheat the air fryer to 375°F (190°C). Place the Brussels sprouts in the air fryer basket in a single layer. Air fry for 10 minutes, shaking the basket halfway through. Add pecan halves to the basket, drizzle with maple syrup, and toss to combine. Continue air frying for an additional 2 minutes or until the Brussels sprouts are golden and the pecans are slightly toasted. Season with salt, pepper, and lemon zest before serving.

NUTRITIONAL INFORMATION

Per serving: 210 calories, 4g protein, 12g carbohydrates, 18g fat, 5g fiber, 0mg cholesterol, 20mg sodium, 450mg potassium.

Spinach & Pine Nut Crunchy Rolls

INGREDIENTS

- 1 cup fresh spinach, finely chopped
- 1/2 cup pine nuts, toasted and roughly chopped
- 1/4 cup nutritional yeast
- 2 garlic cloves, minced
- Salt and pepper, to taste
- 1 tbsp olive oil
- 8 vegan phyllo pastry sheets
- Cooking spray or additional olive oil for brushing

 Prep Time: 20 min

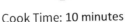 Cook Time: 10 minutes

 Serves: 4

DIRECTIONS

In a medium-sized bowl, combine the chopped spinach, pine nuts, nutritional yeast, minced garlic, olive oil, salt, and pepper. Mix well until all ingredients are thoroughly combined. Lay out one sheet of phyllo on a clean work surface, lightly brush with oil or spray with cooking spray. Place another sheet on top and press gently to stick. Repeat until you have four layers. Place half of the spinach mixture on the lower third of the phyllo stack. Roll up tightly, then cut into three or four smaller rolls. Repeat with remaining ingredients. Preheat the air fryer to 380°F (193°C). Place the rolls in the air fryer basket ensuring they don't overlap. Air fry for 8-10 minutes, turning halfway, or until the rolls are golden brown and crispy.

NUTRITIONAL INFORMATION

Per serving: 280 calories, 8g protein, 24g carbohydrates, 18g fat, 3g fiber, 0mg cholesterol, 180mg sodium, 320mg potassium.

Shrimp and Avocado Summer Rolls

INGREDIENTS

- 1 lb broccolini, washed and ends trimmed
- 2 tbsp olive oil
- Salt and pepper, to taste
- 1/4 cup balsamic vinegar
- 1 tbsp maple syrup or agave nectar
- 1 garlic clove, minced
- Pinch of red pepper flakes (optional)

 Prep Time: 30 min

 Cook Time: 0 minutes

 Serves: 4

DIRECTIONS

In a mixing bowl, toss the broccolini with olive oil, salt, and pepper, ensuring each piece is well coated. Preheat the air fryer to 375°F (190°C). Spread the broccolini in the air fryer basket in a single layer. Air fry for about 8-10 minutes or until tender and slightly crispy, turning halfway through. While the broccolini is cooking, prepare the glaze. In a small saucepan, combine balsamic vinegar, maple syrup or agave nectar, minced garlic, and red pepper flakes. Bring to a simmer and let it reduce for about 5 minutes or until thickened. Once broccolini is done, drizzle the balsamic glaze over it and toss to combine. Serve immediately.

NUTRITIONAL INFORMATION

Per serving: 110 calories, 3g protein, 15g carbohydrates, 5g fat, 3g fiber, 0mg cholesterol, 45mg sodium, 320mg potassium.

Herbed Green Bean Fries

INGREDIENTS

- 1 lb fresh green beans, washed and trimmed
- 2 tbsp olive oil
- 1/2 cup breadcrumbs (use gluten-free if needed)
- 1/4 cup nutritional yeast
- 1 tsp dried basil
- 1 tsp dried oregano
- 1/2 tsp garlic powder
- Salt and pepper, to taste
- Optional dipping sauce: Vegan aioli or tahini sauce

 Prep Time: 15 min

 Cook Time: 10 minutes

 Serves: 4

DIRECTIONS

In a mixing bowl, toss the green beans with olive oil, ensuring they are well-coated. In a separate bowl, mix breadcrumbs, nutritional yeast, dried basil, dried oregano, garlic powder, salt, and pepper. Dip each green bean in the breadcrumb mixture, pressing it onto the beans to ensure they're well coated. Preheat the air fryer to 380°F (193°C). Arrange the coated green beans in a single layer in the air fryer basket, ensuring they're not overcrowded. You might need to cook in batches. Air fry for 8-10 minutes or until golden and crispy. Serve immediately with your choice of vegan dipping sauce.

NUTRITIONAL INFORMATION

Per serving: 160 calories, 6g protein, 22g carbohydrates, 6g fat, 6g fiber, 0mg cholesterol, 100mg sodium, 240mg potassium.

Mustard Maple Kale Crisps

INGREDIENTS

- 1 bunch of kale (roughly 10 large leaves), washed, stemmed, and torn into bite-sized pieces
- 2 tbsp olive oil
- 2 tbsp pure maple syrup
- 1 tbsp Dijon mustard
- 1/2 tsp garlic powder
- Salt, to taste
- Pinch of red pepper flakes (optional)

 Prep Time: 10 min

 Cook Time: 10 minutes

 Serves: 4

DIRECTIONS

In a large bowl, whisk together olive oil, maple syrup, Dijon mustard, garlic powder, salt, and red pepper flakes (if using). Add the torn kale pieces to the bowl and massage the mixture into the kale, ensuring each piece is well-coated. Preheat the air fryer to 375°F (190°C). Arrange the coated kale pieces in a single layer in the air fryer basket, making sure they're not overcrowded. It might be necessary to cook in batches. Air fry for 8-10 minutes or until the edges of the kale are crisp but not burnt. Check halfway and give them a little shake to ensure even cooking.

NUTRITIONAL INFORMATION

Per serving: 90 calories, 2g protein, 11g carbohydrates, 5g fat, 1g fiber, 0mg cholesterol, 95mg sodium, 320mg potassium.

Collard Green Dolmas with Almond Sauce

INGREDIENTS

- 8 large collard green leaves, washed and stems removed
- 1 cup cooked quinoa
- 1/2 cup diced tomatoes (fresh or canned)
- 1/4 cup finely chopped red onion
- 1/4 cup chopped fresh parsley
- 1/4 cup chopped fresh mint
- 1 tbsp olive oil
- 1 tsp lemon zest
- 1/2 cup almond butter
- 2 tbsp lemon juice
- 1 tbsp tamari or soy sauce
- 2 cloves garlic, minced
- 1/4 cup water (or more to desired consistency)

 Prep Time: 20 min

 Cook Time: 10 minutes

 Serves: 4

DIRECTIONS

In a large mixing bowl, combine quinoa, diced tomatoes, red onion, parsley, mint, olive oil, lemon zest, salt, and pepper. Stir until well combined. Lay a collard green leaf flat on a cutting board. Place a generous spoonful of the quinoa mixture at the bottom center of the leaf. Fold in the sides and roll up the leaf, similar to a burrito. Repeat with the remaining leaves and filling. Preheat the air fryer to 360°F (180°C). Place the rolled collard dolmas in a single layer in the air fryer basket, ensuring they're not touching. Air fry for 8-10 minutes, or until the collard greens are tender and slightly crispy. For the almond sauce, blend all ingredients in a food processor or blender until smooth. Serve the dolmas with the sauce on the side.

NUTRITIONAL INFORMATION

Per serving: 280 calories, 9g protein, 27g carbohydrates, 17g fat, 6g fiber, 0mg cholesterol, 320mg sodium, 500mg potassium.

Spicy Chili Bok Choy

INGREDIENTS

- 4 medium-sized bok choy heads, cleaned and cut in half lengthwise
- 2 tbsp sesame oil
- 2 tbsp soy sauce or tamari
- 1 tbsp chili paste or sriracha (adjust according to heat preference)
- 2 garlic cloves, minced
- 1 tbsp ginger, grated
- 1 tbsp sesame seeds (for garnish)
- 2 green onions, thinly sliced (for garnish)

 Prep Time: 10 min

 Cook Time: 8 minutes

 Serves: 4

DIRECTIONS

In a mixing bowl, whisk together sesame oil, soy sauce or tamari, chili paste or sriracha, minced garlic, and grated ginger to form a marinade. Brush each bok choy half generously with the spicy marinade, ensuring all parts are well-coated. Preheat the air fryer to 375°F (190°C). Once heated, place the bok choy halves in the air fryer basket in a single layer, ensuring they're not overlapping.
Air fry for 7-8 minutes, or until the edges of the bok choy are slightly crispy and golden. Serve immediately, garnished with sesame seeds and sliced green onions.

NUTRITIONAL INFORMATION

Per serving: 90 calories, 3g protein, 7g carbohydrates, 6g fat, 2g fiber, 0mg cholesterol, 600mg sodium, 400mg potassium.

Crunchy Romaine & Radish Salad

INGREDIENTS

- 2 heads of romaine lettuce, washed and roughly chopped
- 8-10 radishes, thinly sliced
- 1 cup croutons (air-fried, made from whole grain bread cubes)
- 1 tbsp olive oil
- 1 tsp garlic powder
- Salt and pepper to taste

Dressing:
- 3 tbsp olive oil
- 2 tbsp apple cider vinegar
- 1 tsp Dijon mustard
- 1 garlic clove, minced
- Salt and pepper to taste

 Prep Time: 15 min   Cook Time: 5 minutes   Serves: 4

DIRECTIONS

To make the croutons, toss the bread cubes in olive oil, garlic powder, salt, and pepper. Preheat the air fryer to 375°F (190°C). Place the bread cubes in the air fryer basket in a single layer and air fry for 5 minutes, or until they're golden and crispy. In a large salad bowl, combine the chopped romaine lettuce and thinly sliced radishes. Prepare the dressing by whisking together olive oil, apple cider vinegar, Dijon mustard, minced garlic, salt, and pepper in a small bowl.

Pour the dressing over the romaine and radish mixture and toss until well combined. Top the salad with the crunchy croutons. Serve immediately.

NUTRITIONAL INFORMATION

Per serving: 140 calories, 3g protein, 12g carbohydrates, 10g fat, 4g fiber, 0mg cholesterol, 120mg sodium, 340mg potassium.

Garlic Parmesan Swiss Chard

INGREDIENTS

- 1 large bunch of Swiss chard, stems removed and leaves chopped
- 2 tbsp olive oil
- 3 garlic cloves, minced
- 1/4 cup vegan Parmesan cheese, grated
- 1/4 tsp red pepper flakes (optional)
- Salt and pepper to taste

 Prep Time: 10 min   Cook Time: 8 minutes   Serves: 4

DIRECTIONS

Preheat the air fryer to 375°F (190°C). In a large bowl, toss the Swiss chard leaves with olive oil, minced garlic, red pepper flakes (if using), and a pinch of salt and pepper until well coated. Transfer the coated Swiss chard to the air fryer basket, spreading it out evenly. Air fry for about 8 minutes, shaking the basket halfway through, or until the leaves are crispy and slightly browned. Once cooked, transfer the Swiss chard to a serving plate and sprinkle with vegan Parmesan cheese. Toss gently to combine and serve immediately.

NUTRITIONAL INFORMATION

Per serving: 90 calories, 3g protein, 7g carbohydrates, 6g fat, 2g fiber, 0mg cholesterol, 210mg sodium, 420mg potassium..

Asian Sesame Spinach Chips

INGREDIENTS

- 1 large bunch of fresh spinach, washed and thoroughly dried
- 2 tbsp sesame oil
- 1 tbsp low-sodium soy sauce or tamari (for gluten-free option)
- 1 tbsp toasted sesame seeds
- 1/2 tsp garlic powder
- 1/4 tsp ground ginger

Prep Time: 10 min

Cook Time: 6 minutes

Serves: 4

DIRECTIONS

Preheat the air fryer to 350°F (175°C). In a large mixing bowl, whisk together sesame oil, soy sauce or tamari, garlic powder, and ground ginger. Gently toss the spinach leaves in the mixture until they are evenly coated. Place the coated spinach leaves in a single layer in the air fryer basket, ensuring they don't overlap. Air fry for 6 minutes or until crisp, checking halfway through to ensure they don't burn. Once done, sprinkle the chips with toasted sesame seeds.

NUTRITIONAL INFORMATION

Per serving: 70 calories, 2g protein, 3g carbohydrates, 6g fat, 2g fiber, 0mg cholesterol, 150mg sodium, 240mg potassium.

Herb-Infused Endive Bites

INGREDIENTS

- 4 large Belgian endives, separated into leaves and washed
- 2 tbsp olive oil
- 1 tsp dried thyme
- 1 tsp dried rosemary
- 1 tsp dried oregano
- 1/4 tsp garlic powder
- Salt and pepper, to taste
- 2 tbsp chopped fresh parsley (for garnish)

Prep Time: 15 min

Cook Time: 10 minutes

Serves: 4

DIRECTIONS

Preheat the air fryer to 375°F (190°C). In a large mixing bowl, whisk together olive oil, thyme, rosemary, oregano, garlic powder, salt, and pepper. Gently toss the endive leaves in the herb mixture until they're evenly coated. Arrange the coated endive leaves in a single layer in the air fryer basket. Air fry for 10 minutes or until the edges are slightly crispy. Remove from the air fryer, plate, and sprinkle with chopped fresh parsley before serving.

NUTRITIONAL INFORMATION

Per serving: 60 calories, 1g protein, 5g carbohydrates, 4g fat, 3g fiber, 0mg cholesterol, 25mg sodium, 320mg potassium.

Tangy Air-Fried Cabbage Steaks

INGREDIENTS

- 1 medium-sized head of green cabbage, sliced into 1-inch thick steaks
- 2 tbsp olive oil
- 1 tbsp apple cider vinegar
- 1 tsp Dijon mustard
- Salt and pepper, to taste
- 1 tsp smoked paprika
- 1 tbsp chopped fresh dill (for garnish)

Prep Time: 10 min

Cook Time: 14 minutes

Serves: 4

DIRECTIONS

In a small bowl, whisk together olive oil, apple cider vinegar, Dijon mustard, smoked paprika, salt, and pepper. Brush each cabbage steak on both sides with the tangy mixture. Preheat the air fryer to 375°F (190°C). Place the cabbage steaks in a single layer in the air fryer basket. Air fry for 7 minutes on each side or until the edges are crispy and golden. Once cooked, plate the cabbage steaks and garnish with fresh dill.

NUTRITIONAL INFORMATION

Per serving: 85 calories, 2g protein, 10g carbohydrates, 5g fat, 4g fiber, 0mg cholesterol, 50mg sodium, 300mg potassium.

Crispy Caesar Salad Cups

INGREDIENTS

- 4 large vegan tortillas
- 4 cups Romaine lettuce, chopped
- 1/2 cup vegan Caesar dressing
- 1/4 cup vegan parmesan cheese, grated
- 1 cup cherry tomatoes, halved
- 1/2 cup croutons (ensure vegan-friendly)
- 2 tbsp olive oil
- 1 tbsp lemon juice
- Salt and pepper, to taste

Prep Time: 20 min

Cook Time: 10 minutes

Serves: 4

DIRECTIONS

Using a large round cutter or a bowl as a guide, cut out large circles from the vegan tortillas. Lightly brush each side of the tortilla circles with olive oil. Gently press each tortilla circle into the cups of an upside-down muffin tin to form a cup shape. Preheat the air fryer to 350°F (175°C). Place the muffin tin with tortilla cups in the air fryer and cook for 8-10 minutes or until they are crispy and hold their shape. Allow them to cool. In a large bowl, toss together the Romaine lettuce, cherry tomatoes, croutons, vegan Caesar dressing, lemon juice, salt, and pepper. Fill each crispy tortilla cup with the Caesar salad mixture, top with vegan parmesan cheese, and serve immediately.

NUTRITIONAL INFORMATION

Per serving: 280 calories, 7g protein, 32g carbohydrates, 15g fat, 3g fiber, 0mg cholesterol, 540mg sodium, 220mg potassium.

Roots & Tubers

Sweet Potato & Cinnamon Fries

INGREDIENTS

- 2 large sweet potatoes, peeled and sliced into fries
- 2 tbsp olive oil
- 2 tsp ground cinnamon
- Salt to taste
- Optional: 1 tbsp maple syrup for a touch of sweetness

 Prep Time: 10 min

 Cook Time: 15 minutes

 Serves: 4

DIRECTIONS

In a large bowl, toss the sweet potato fries with olive oil, ground cinnamon, and salt. If using, drizzle with maple syrup and toss until well coated. Preheat the air fryer to 390°F (200°C). Arrange the sweet potato fries in a single layer in the air fryer basket, ensuring they don't overlap. Air fry for about 15 minutes, shaking the basket halfway through cooking, until the fries are crispy and golden brown.

NUTRITIONAL INFORMATION

Per serving: 180 calories, 2g protein, 34g carbohydrates, 5g fat, 5g fiber, 0mg cholesterol, 65mg sodium, 440mg potassium.

Rosemary Roasted Air-Fried Beets

INGREDIENTS

- 4 medium beets, peeled and sliced into 1/4-inch rounds
- 2 tbsp olive oil
- 2 tsp fresh rosemary, finely chopped
- Salt and black pepper, to taste

 Prep Time: 10 min

 Cook Time: 20 minutes

 Serves: 4

DIRECTIONS

In a mixing bowl, combine beet slices, olive oil, rosemary, salt, and black pepper. Toss until all beet slices are well coated. Preheat the air fryer to 375°F (190°C). Arrange the beet slices in a single layer in the air fryer basket, avoiding overlap. Air fry for 20 minutes, turning the beets halfway through, or until they are tender and have crispy edges.

NUTRITIONAL INFORMATION

Per serving: 110 calories, 2g protein, 16g carbohydrates, 5g fat, 4g fiber, 0mg cholesterol, 80mg sodium, 500mg potassium.

Spicy Curried Parsnip Fries

INGREDIENTS

- 4 large parsnips, peeled and cut into fry-like strips
- 2 tbsp olive oil
- 2 tsp curry powder
- 1/2 tsp cayenne pepper (adjust to your heat preference)
- Salt, to taste
- Fresh cilantro, for garnish (optional)

 Prep Time: 15 minutes

 Cook Time: 20 minutes

 Serves: 4

DIRECTIONS

In a large mixing bowl, combine the parsnip strips, olive oil, curry powder, cayenne pepper, and salt. Toss well to ensure that the parsnips are evenly coated with the spices and oil. Preheat the air fryer to 375°F (190°C). Arrange the spiced parsnip strips in a single layer in the air fryer basket. It's best to avoid overcrowding, so you might need to cook in batches depending on the size of your air fryer. Cook for 20 minutes, turning halfway through, until the parsnip fries are golden brown and crispy. Once done, transfer to a serving dish and garnish with fresh cilantro if desired.

NUTRITIONAL INFORMATION

Per serving: 140 calories, 2g protein, 27g carbohydrates, 5g fat, 6g fiber, 0mg cholesterol, 80mg sodium, 500mg potassium.

Garlic & Herb Turnip Tots

INGREDIENTS

- 4 medium turnips, peeled and grated
- 2 garlic cloves, minced
- 2 tbsp fresh parsley, finely chopped
- 1 tbsp fresh chives, finely chopped
- 2 tbsp nutritional yeast (gives a cheesy flavor without dairy)
- 1 tbsp olive oil
- Salt and black pepper, to taste
- 1/4 cup flaxseed meal (to bind)

 Prep Time: 20 min

 Cook Time: 15 minutes

 Serves: 4

DIRECTIONS

In a large mixing bowl, combine grated turnips, minced garlic, parsley, chives, nutritional yeast, olive oil, flaxseed meal, salt, and black pepper. Mix thoroughly until the mixture is well combined. Shape the mixture into small tot shapes with your hands, pressing firmly to ensure they hold together. Preheat the air fryer to 375°F (190°C). Place the turnip tots in a single layer, ensuring they don't touch. Cook for 15 minutes, turning halfway through, or until the tots are golden brown and crispy on the outside. Serve hot, with your favorite dipping sauce if desired.

NUTRITIONAL INFORMATION

Per serving: 110 calories, 4g protein, 14g carbohydrates, 5g fat, 4g fiber, 0mg cholesterol, 50mg sodium, 300mg potassium.

Crispy Radish & Dill Bites

INGREDIENTS

- 2 cups radishes, thinly sliced
- 2 tbsp fresh dill, finely chopped
- 1 tbsp olive oil
- 1 tsp lemon zest
- Salt and black pepper, to taste
- 2 tbsp almond flour (for added crispiness)

 Prep Time: 15 min

 Cook Time: 12 minutes

 Serves: 4

DIRECTIONS

In a mixing bowl, combine sliced radishes, dill, olive oil, lemon zest, almond flour, salt, and pepper. Toss until radishes are well-coated. Preheat the air fryer to 375°F (190°C). Evenly spread the radish slices in a single layer in the fryer basket, ensuring they don't overlap. Cook for 12 minutes, shaking or turning the slices halfway through, until they are crispy and golden. Transfer to a serving dish, sprinkle with additional fresh dill if desired, and serve immediately as a snack or side dish.

NUTRITIONAL INFORMATION

Per serving: 65 calories, 2g protein, 4g carbohydrates, 5g fat, 2g fiber, 0mg cholesterol, 60mg sodium, 230mg potassium.

Golden Brown Cassava Chips

INGREDIENTS

- 2 medium cassava roots, peeled and thinly sliced
- 2 tbsp olive oil
- Salt, to taste
- Optional: A pinch of paprika or cayenne for some kick

 Prep Time: 10 min

 Cook Time: 15 minutes

 Serves: 4

DIRECTIONS

After peeling and slicing the cassava, soak the slices in cold water for about 10 minutes to remove excess starch. This will help them crisp up in the air fryer. Drain and pat dry with a kitchen towel. In a mixing bowl, combine the cassava slices, olive oil, salt, and optional spices. Toss until the slices are well-coated with the oil. Preheat the air fryer to 375°F (190°C). Arrange the cassava slices in a single layer in the fryer basket, ensuring they don't overlap. Cook for 15 minutes, turning or shaking the slices halfway through, until they turn golden brown and crispy. Serve immediately as a snack or side dish.

NUTRITIONAL INFORMATION

Per serving: 210 calories, 1.5g protein, 50g carbohydrates, 7g fat, 3g fiber, 0mg cholesterol, 15mg sodium, 330mg potassium.

Lemon Zested Carrot Crisps

INGREDIENTS

- 4 large carrots, peeled and sliced thinly into rounds
- 2 tbsp olive oil
- Zest of 1 lemon
- Salt, to taste
- A pinch of black pepper
- Optional: fresh parsley or dill for garnish

 Prep Time: 15 min

 Cook Time: 12 minutes

 Serves: 4

DIRECTIONS

In a mixing bowl, combine the thinly sliced carrots, olive oil, lemon zest, salt, and black pepper. Toss until the carrot slices are well-coated. Preheat the air fryer to 375°F (190°C). Arrange the carrot slices in a single layer in the fryer basket, ensuring they don't overlap. Cook for 12 minutes, turning the slices halfway through, until they are crispy and have a golden hue. Garnish with optional fresh herbs and serve immediately as a delightful snack or side dish.

NUTRITIONAL INFORMATION

Per serving: 90 calories, 1g protein, 12g carbohydrates, 4.5g fat, 3g fiber, 0mg cholesterol, 70mg sodium, 290mg potassium.

Thyme and Sea Salt Jicama Sticks

INGREDIENTS

- 1 large jicama, peeled and cut into sticks (similar to the size of thick fries)
- 1 tbsp olive oil
- 1 tsp dried thyme (or 1 tbsp fresh thyme, chopped)
- 1 tsp coarse sea salt
- A pinch of black pepper

 Prep Time: 10 min

Cook Time: 15 minutes

 Serves: 4

DIRECTIONS

In a large mixing bowl, toss the jicama sticks with olive oil, thyme, sea salt, and black pepper, ensuring they're evenly coated. Preheat the air fryer to 375°F (190°C). Place the jicama sticks in a single layer in the fryer basket without overcrowding. Cook for 15 minutes, giving them a shake or stir halfway through, until they're slightly crispy on the outside and tender on the inside. Serve immediately as a refreshing and unique side dish or snack.

NUTRITIONAL INFORMATION

Per serving: 70 calories, 1g protein, 16g carbohydrates, 3.5g fat, 8g fiber, 0mg cholesterol, 590mg sodium, 220mg potassium.

Roasted Red Potato Wedges with Chive Dip

INGREDIENTS

For the Potato Wedges:

- 4 large red potatoes, washed and cut into wedges
- 2 tbsp olive oil
- 1 tsp paprika
- 1/2 tsp garlic powder
- Salt and pepper, to taste

For the Chive Dip:

- 1 cup unsweetened plant-based yogurt (e.g., almond, soy, or coconut)
- 2 tbsp fresh chives, finely chopped
- 1 clove garlic, minced
- 1 tsp lemon juice
- Salt and pepper, to taste

Prep Time: 10 minutes

Cook Time: 20 minutes

Serves: 4

DIRECTIONS

In a large bowl, toss the potato wedges with olive oil, paprika, garlic powder, salt, and pepper until evenly coated. Preheat the air fryer to 390°F (200°C). Arrange the potato wedges in the air fryer basket in a single layer, ensuring not to overcrowd them. Air fry for 20 minutes, shaking the basket halfway through, until the wedges are golden brown and crispy. While the potatoes are cooking, mix together the plant-based yogurt, chives, minced garlic, lemon juice, salt, and pepper in a bowl. Refrigerate until ready to serve. Serve the roasted potato wedges hot with the chilled chive dip.

NUTRITIONAL INFORMATION

Per serving: 230 calories, 5g protein, 40g carbohydrates, 6g fat, 4g fiber, 0mg cholesterol, 120mg sodium, 960mg potassium.

Air-Fried Ginger & Soy Glazed Rutabaga

INGREDIENTS

- 2 large rutabagas, peeled and cut into 1/2-inch thick sticks
- 2 tbsp olive oil
- 2 tbsp soy sauce (low sodium)
- 1 tbsp maple syrup or agave nectar
- 1-inch piece of fresh ginger, grated
- 2 cloves garlic, minced
- 1 tsp toasted sesame oil
- 1 tbsp sesame seeds (for garnish)
- 2 green onions, thinly sliced (for garnish)

Prep Time: 15 min

Cook Time: 20 minutes

Serves: 4

DIRECTIONS

In a large mixing bowl, whisk together the olive oil, soy sauce, maple syrup, grated ginger, minced garlic, and sesame oil. Add the rutabaga sticks to the bowl and toss to coat them evenly with the mixture. Preheat the air fryer to 375°F (190°C). Arrange the rutabaga sticks in the air fryer basket in a single layer, ensuring not to overcrowd them. Air fry for 20 minutes, shaking the basket occasionally, until the rutabaga sticks are tender and have a nice caramelized glaze. Serve hot, garnished with sesame seeds and sliced green onions.

NUTRITIONAL INFORMATION

Per serving: 190 calories, 3g protein, 30g carbohydrates, 7g fat, 6g fiber, 0mg cholesterol, 380mg sodium, 560mg potassium.

Harissa Spiced Daikon Medallions

INGREDIENTS

- 1 large daikon radish, peeled and sliced into 1/2-inch thick medallions
- 2 tbsp olive oil
- 1 tbsp harissa paste
- 1 garlic clove, minced
- 1/2 tsp ground cumin
- Salt to taste
- Freshly chopped cilantro or parsley, for garnish

Prep Time: 10 min

Cook Time: 18 minutes

Serves: 4

DIRECTIONS

In a mixing bowl, combine olive oil, harissa paste, minced garlic, cumin, and salt. Stir to form a smooth marinade. Add the daikon medallions to the bowl and toss to coat them evenly in the harissa mixture. Preheat the air fryer to 375°F (190°C). Arrange the coated daikon medallions in the air fryer basket in a single layer. Air fry for 18 minutes, turning the medallions halfway through, until they're golden brown and slightly crispy. Garnish with chopped cilantro or parsley before serving.

NUTRITIONAL INFORMATION

Per serving: 95 calories, 1g protein, 7g carbohydrates, 7g fat, 2g fiber, 0mg cholesterol, 250mg sodium, 270mg potassium.

Turmeric & Lime Yucca Fries

INGREDIENTS

- 1 large yucca root, peeled and cut into fries
- 2 tbsp olive oil
- Zest and juice of 1 lime
- 1 tsp ground turmeric
- Salt to taste
- 1 tbsp fresh cilantro, chopped (optional for garnish)

Prep Time: 15 minutes

Cook Time: 20 minutes

Serves: 4

DIRECTIONS

In a large bowl, whisk together olive oil, lime zest, lime juice, turmeric, and salt.
Add the yucca fries to the bowl and toss them until they're well-coated with the mixture. Preheat the air fryer to 375°F (190°C). Once heated, arrange the yucca fries in the basket in a single layer, ensuring they aren't crowded. Air fry for 20 minutes, turning the fries halfway through the cook time, until they're golden brown and crispy on the edges. Garnish with fresh cilantro before serving, if desired.

NUTRITIONAL INFORMATION

Per serving: 200 calories, 2g protein, 40g carbohydrates, 5g fat, 3g fiber, 0mg cholesterol, 10mg sodium, 500mg potassium.

Balsamic Glazed Onion Petals

INGREDIENTS

- 2 large red onions, peeled and cut into petals
- 3 tbsp olive oil
- Salt to taste
- Black pepper to taste
- 4 tbsp balsamic reduction/glaze

Prep Time: 10 min

Cook Time: 15 minutes

Serves: 4

DIRECTIONS

In a mixing bowl, combine the onion petals, olive oil, salt, and black pepper. Toss to ensure each petal is well-coated. Preheat the air fryer to 375°F (190°C). Once heated, place the onion petals in a single layer in the air fryer basket. Air fry for 15 minutes, turning them halfway, until they're tender and have a slight char. Once done, transfer the onion petals to a serving plate and drizzle with balsamic reduction/glaze.

NUTRITIONAL INFORMATION

Per serving: 125 calories, 1g protein, 15g carbohydrates, 7g fat, 2g fiber, 0mg cholesterol, 5mg sodium, 180mg potassium.

Toasted Garlic & Parsley Jerusalem Artichokes

INGREDIENTS

- 1 lb Jerusalem artichokes (sunchokes), washed and thinly sliced
- 4 garlic cloves, finely minced
- 3 tbsp olive oil
- Salt to taste
- Black pepper to taste
- 3 tbsp fresh parsley, finely chopped

Prep Time: 10 min

Cook Time: 20 minutes

Serves: 4

DIRECTIONS

In a mixing bowl, combine the sliced Jerusalem artichokes, minced garlic, olive oil, salt, and pepper. Toss well to coat the slices evenly. Preheat the air fryer to 375°F (190°C). Once heated, arrange the Jerusalem artichokes in a single layer in the air fryer basket. Air fry for 20 minutes, turning halfway through, or until they are golden brown and crispy. Transfer the toasted Jerusalem artichokes to a serving dish, sprinkle with fresh parsley, and serve immediately.

NUTRITIONAL INFORMATION

Per serving: 180 calories, 3g protein, 29g carbohydrates, 7g fat, 5g fiber, 0mg cholesterol, 20mg sodium, 450mg potassium.

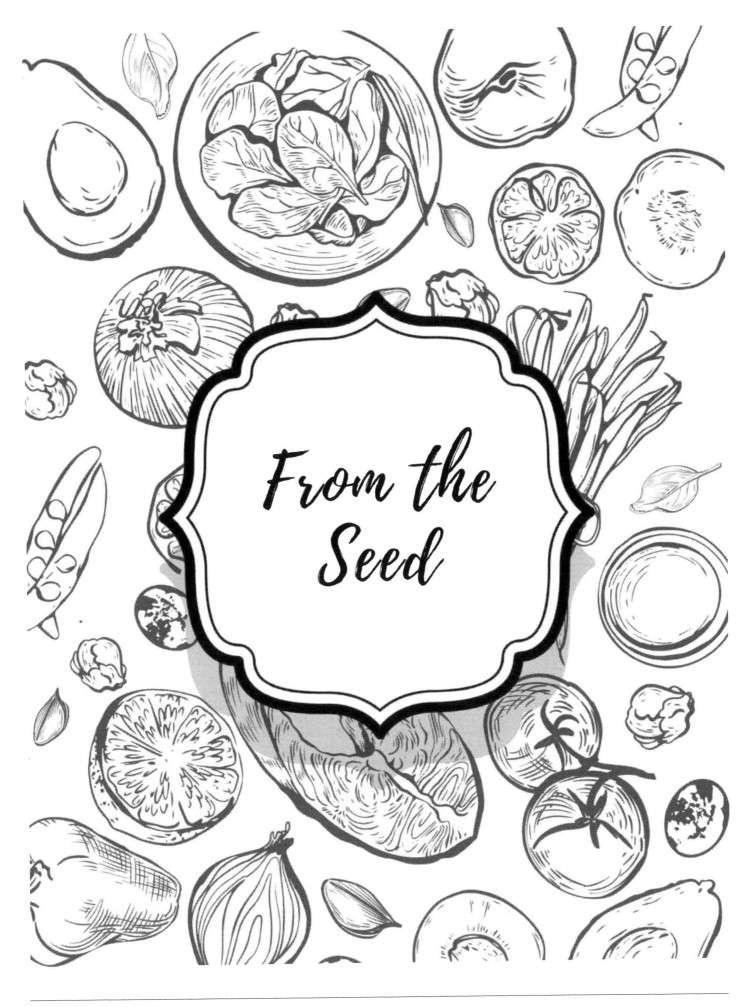

From the
Seed

Spicy Lentil Meatballs

INGREDIENTS

- 2 cups cooked green lentils
- 1 small onion, finely chopped
- 2 garlic cloves, minced
- 2 tbsp ground flaxseed mixed with 5 tbsp water (as a binder)
- 1/2 cup breadcrumbs
- 2 tbsp tomato paste
- 1 tsp smoked paprika
- 1 tsp cumin
- 1/2 tsp chili flakes (adjust to taste)
- Salt to taste
- 2 tbsp fresh cilantro, finely chopped
- 1 tbsp olive oil

 Prep Time: 15 minutes

 Cook Time: 20 minutes

 Serves: 4

DIRECTIONS

In a food processor, blend the lentils, onion, garlic, flaxseed mixture, breadcrumbs, tomato paste, smoked paprika, cumin, chili flakes, and salt until well combined but not pureed. Transfer the mixture to a bowl and fold in the cilantro. Form the mixture into small meatball-sized balls, slightly oiling your hands if the mixture sticks. Preheat the air fryer to 375°F (190°C). Lightly brush the meatballs with olive oil and place them in a single layer in the air fryer basket. Air fry for 20 minutes, turning halfway through, until they are golden brown and firm to the touch.

NUTRITIONAL INFORMATION

Per serving: 220 calories, 12g protein, 35g carbohydrates, 4g fat, 10g fiber, 0mg cholesterol, 180mg sodium, 550mg potassium.

Black Bean & Corn Empanadas

INGREDIENTS

- 1 cup cooked and mashed black beans
- 1/2 cup corn kernels (fresh or frozen)
- 1 small onion, finely chopped
- 1 red bell pepper, diced
- 1 clove garlic, minced
- 2 tbsp fresh cilantro, chopped
- 1 tsp ground cumin
- Salt and pepper to taste
- 1 tbsp olive oil, plus extra for brushing
- 1 pack vegan empanada dough (store-bought or homemade)

 Prep Time: 25 min

 Cook Time: 15 minutes

 Serves: 4

DIRECTIONS

Heat olive oil in a skillet, sauté onion, bell pepper, and garlic until softened. Add black beans, corn, cumin, salt, and pepper. Cook for 3 minutes, stir in cilantro, and remove from heat. Roll out empanada dough, cut into circles, and fill each with the black bean mixture. Fold into a half-moon shape, press edges with a fork to seal. Preheat air fryer to 350°F, brush empanadas with olive oil, and cook for 15 minutes until golden brown, turning halfway for even cooking.

NUTRITIONAL INFORMATION

Per serving: 320 calories, 9g protein, 50g carbohydrates, 10g fat, 7g fiber, 0mg cholesterol, 210mg sodium, 400mg potassium.

Air-Fried Falafel with Tahini Drizzle

INGREDIENTS

- 1 cup dried chickpeas, soaked overnight and drained
- 1 small onion, chopped
- 2-3 garlic cloves, minced
- 1/4 cup fresh parsley, cilantro, chopped
- 1 tsp ground cumin, coriander
- 1/4 tsp chili powder (optional)
- 1/2 tsp baking soda
- 2 tbsp chickpea flour (or as needed), olive oil, for brushing
- 1/4 cup tahini
- 2 tbsp lemon juice, water
- 1 clove garlic, minced

 Prep Time: 20 minutes

  Cook Time: 15 minutes

 Serves: 4

DIRECTIONS

In a food processor, combine the soaked chickpeas, onion, garlic, parsley, cilantro, cumin, coriander, chili powder, salt, and pepper. Process until almost smooth, but still slightly chunky. Transfer the mixture to a bowl, add baking soda and chickpea flour. Mix until the mixture holds together when shaped. Form into small balls or patties. Preheat the air fryer to 375°F (190°C). Brush each falafel with a bit of olive oil and place them in a single layer in the air fryer basket. Cook for 15 minutes, turning halfway through, until golden brown and crispy. While the falafel is cooking, mix together all the ingredients for the tahini drizzle in a small bowl. Serve the hot falafel drizzled with the tahini sauce.

NUTRITIONAL INFORMATION

Per serving: 270 calories, 10g protein, 35g carbohydrates, 11g fat, 9g fiber, 0mg cholesterol, 300mg sodium, 500mg potassium.

Crispy Chickpea & Quinoa Patties

INGREDIENTS

- 1 cup cooked quinoa
- 1 can (15 oz) chickpeas, drained and rinsed
- 2 garlic cloves, minced
- 2 tbsp chopped fresh parsley
- 1 tbsp olive oil or tahini (for binding)
- 1/2 tsp smoked paprika, cumin
- 1/4 cup finely chopped red bell pepper
- 2 tbsp flaxseed meal mixed with 5 tbsp water (acts as flax "egg")
- Optional: 2 tbsp nutritional yeast (for a cheesy flavor)

 Prep Time: 20 min

 Cook Time: 15 minutes

 Serves: 4

DIRECTIONS

In a food processor, blend chickpeas, garlic, parsley, olive oil/tahini, smoked paprika, cumin, salt, pepper, and optional nutritional yeast. Transfer to a bowl, add cooked quinoa, chopped red bell pepper, and flax "egg". Mix, shape into small patties, ensuring even thickness. Preheat air fryer to 375°F, cook patties for 15 minutes, flipping halfway, until golden brown and crispy. Serve hot with your preferred sauce or dip.

NUTRITIONAL INFORMATION

Per serving: 230 calories, 10g protein, 35g carbohydrates, 6g fat, 7g fiber, 0mg cholesterol, 300mg sodium, 400mg potassium.

Spiced Pinto Bean Taquitos

INGREDIENTS

- 1 can (15 oz) pinto beans, drained and rinsed
- 1/2 cup red onion, finely chopped
- 2 garlic cloves, minced
- 1 jalapeño, deseeded and finely chopped (optional for extra heat)
- 1 tsp ground cumin
- 1/2 tsp smoked paprika
- Salt and black pepper to taste
- 8 small corn tortillas
- 1 tbsp olive oil (for brushing)
- 1/2 cup vegan cheese shreds (optional)

Prep Time: 15 min

Cook Time: 10 minutes

Serves: 4

DIRECTIONS

Mash pinto beans in a bowl, add red onion, garlic, jalapeño (optional), cumin, smoked paprika, vegan cheese (optional), salt, and black pepper. Mix well. Warm tortillas, spoon 2 tbsp of the mixture onto each, roll tightly, and brush with olive oil. Preheat air fryer to 400°F, place taquitos seam-side down without touching, and cook for 10 minutes until golden and crispy. Serve immediately, garnished with cilantro and lime wedges if desired.

NUTRITIONAL INFORMATION

Per serving: 220 calories, 8g protein, 40g carbohydrates, 4g fat, 7g fiber, 0mg cholesterol, 380mg sodium, 450mg potassium.

Sunflower Seed & Herb Croquettes

INGREDIENTS

- 1 cup sunflower seeds, roasted and unsalted
- 1/2 cup fresh parsley, finely chopped
- 1/4 cup fresh chives, finely chopped
- 2 garlic cloves, minced
- 1/2 cup breadcrumbs (preferably whole wheat or gluten-free)
- 1 tbsp flaxseed meal (mixed with 2.5 tbsp water to create a flax "egg")

Prep Time: 20 min

Cook Time: 15 minutes

Serves: 4

DIRECTIONS

In a food processor, blend sunflower seeds, parsley, chives, garlic, half of the breadcrumbs, nutritional yeast (optional), and flax "egg" until textured. Shape into patties, coat with remaining breadcrumbs, and lightly brush with olive oil. Preheat air fryer to 375°F, cook croquettes for 15 minutes, flipping halfway, until golden and crispy. Serve immediately with lemon wedges.

NUTRITIONAL INFORMATION

Per serving: 250 calories, 9g protein, 18g carbohydrates, 17g fat, 4g fiber, 0mg cholesterol, 120mg sodium, 280mg potassium.

Pine Nut & Basil Stuffed Peppers

INGREDIENTS

- 4 medium bell peppers (red, yellow, or green)
- 1 cup pine nuts, toasted
- 1 cup cooked quinoa
- 1/2 cup fresh basil, finely chopped
- 2 garlic cloves, minced
- 1/4 cup nutritional yeast (optional for a cheesy flavor)
- 1 tbsp olive oil, plus extra for brushing
- 1/2 cup diced tomatoes (fresh or canned)
- Lemon wedges for serving

Prep Time: 20 min

Cook Time: 25 minutes

Serves: 4

DIRECTIONS

Cut the tops off the bell peppers and remove the seeds and membranes. Set aside. In a mixing bowl, combine toasted pine nuts, cooked quinoa, fresh basil, garlic, nutritional yeast, diced tomatoes, and olive oil. Season with salt and pepper and mix well. Stuff each bell pepper with the pine nut and basil mixture, pressing down to pack the filling. Brush the outside of the peppers with a little olive oil. This helps in getting a roasted texture. Preheat the air fryer to 360°F (182°C). Place the stuffed peppers in the air fryer basket. Cook for 25 minutes or until the peppers are tender and slightly charred. Serve immediately with lemon wedges on the side.

NUTRITIONAL INFORMATION

Per serving: 320 calories, 9g protein, 30g carbohydrates, 20g fat, 6g fiber, 0mg cholesterol, 80mg sodium, 500mg potassium.

Crispy Lemon Dill Chickpeas

INGREDIENTS

- 2 cups cooked chickpeas (or 1 can, drained and rinsed)
- Zest and juice of 1 large lemon
- 2 tbsp olive oil
- 2 tsp dried dill (or 1 tbsp fresh dill, finely chopped)
- Salt and pepper to taste
- 1 tsp garlic powder
- 1/2 tsp onion powder

Prep Time: 10 min

Cook Time: 15 minutes

Serves: 4

DIRECTIONS

In a mixing bowl, combine lemon zest, lemon juice, olive oil, dill, garlic powder, onion powder, salt, and pepper. Mix well. Add the chickpeas to the bowl and toss until they are evenly coated with the lemon-dill mixture. Preheat the air fryer to 375°F (190°C). Spread the chickpeas in a single layer in the air fryer basket. Cook for 15 minutes, shaking the basket every 5 minutes to ensure even cooking, until the chickpeas are crispy and golden. Serve immediately as a snack or salad topping.

NUTRITIONAL INFORMATION

Per serving: 210 calories, 8g protein, 24g carbohydrates, 10g fat, 7g fiber, 0mg cholesterol, 300mg sodium, 400mg potassium.

Adzuki Bean & Mushroom Dumplings

INGREDIENTS

- 1 cup cooked adzuki beans, mashed
- 1 cup finely chopped mushrooms (shiitake or cremini work well)
- 2 green onions, finely chopped
- 2 cloves garlic, minced
- 1 tbsp soy sauce (or tamari for gluten-free)
- 1 tsp toasted sesame oil
- 1/4 cup chopped fresh cilantro
- 1 tsp grated ginger
- 16 vegan dumpling wrappers

 Prep Time: 25 min

 Cook Time: 15 minutes

 Serves: 4

DIRECTIONS

In a large bowl, combine mashed adzuki beans, mushrooms, green onions, garlic, soy sauce, sesame oil, cilantro, ginger, salt, and pepper. Mix until all ingredients are well combined. Take one dumpling wrapper, spoon about a tablespoon of the mixture into the center, fold, and seal the edges. Repeat with the remaining wrappers and filling. Preheat the air fryer to 375°F (190°C). Lightly oil the basket or use a parchment liner. Place dumplings in a single layer, ensuring they don't touch. Air fry for 15 minutes, flipping halfway, or until the dumplings are golden brown and crispy. Serve with dipping sauce of choice.

NUTRITIONAL INFORMATION

Per serving: 200 calories, 8g protein, 35g carbohydrates, 2g fat, 5g fiber, 0mg cholesterol, 450mg sodium, 350mg potassium.

Pumpkin Seed Pesto Pasta Pouches

INGREDIENTS

- 1 cup pumpkin seeds, toasted
- 1 cup fresh basil leaves
- 2 cloves garlic
- 1/4 cup nutritional yeast
- 1/4 cup olive oil
- Salt and pepper to taste
- 16 vegan wonton wrappers or pasta sheets
- 1/2 cup water for sealing

 Prep Time: 30 min

 Cook Time: 15 minutes

Serves: 4

DIRECTIONS

In a food processor, combine toasted pumpkin seeds, basil, garlic, nutritional yeast, olive oil, salt, and pepper. Blend until smooth to make the pesto. Lay out each vegan wonton wrapper or pasta sheet on a clean surface. Spoon about a tablespoon of the pumpkin seed pesto in the center of each. Dampen the edges of the wrapper with water, fold over to create a half-moon shape, and press to seal. Preheat the air fryer to 375°F (190°C). Place the pasta pouches in the fryer basket, ensuring they don't overlap, and air fry for 15 minutes or until they turn golden brown and crispy. Serve immediately with additional pesto or a sauce of choice.

NUTRITIONAL INFORMATION

Per serving: 280 calories, 10g protein, 25g carbohydrates, 16g fat, 3g fiber, 0mg cholesterol, 200mg sodium, 220mg potassium.

Air Fryer Lima Bean Fritters

INGREDIENTS

- 2 cups cooked lima beans
- 1/2 cup breadcrumbs
- 1/4 cup fresh parsley, chopped
- 2 green onions, finely chopped
- 1 clove garlic, minced
- 1 flaxseed "egg" (1 tbsp ground flaxseed mixed with 2.5 tbsp water, let sit for 5 minutes)
- 1/2 tsp cumin
- Salt and pepper to taste
- Olive oil spray for cooking

Prep Time: 15 min   Cook Time: 20 minutes   Serves: 4

DIRECTIONS

In a food processor, combine lima beans, breadcrumbs, parsley, green onions, garlic, flaxseed "egg", cumin, salt, and pepper. Pulse until the mixture is combined but still slightly chunky. Shape the mixture into small patties with your hands. Preheat the air fryer to 375°F (190°C). Lightly spray the fryer basket with olive oil. Place the fritters in the basket in a single layer, ensuring they don't overlap. Lightly spray the tops with olive oil. Air fry for 20 minutes or until golden brown, flipping halfway through. Serve hot with your favorite dipping sauce.

NUTRITIONAL INFORMATION

Per serving: 210 calories, 8g protein, 38g carbohydrates, 3g fat, 7g fiber, 0mg cholesterol, 160mg sodium, 480mg potassium.

Southwest Chia & Bean Quesadillas

INGREDIENTS

- 8 plant-based tortillas
- 1 can (15 oz) black beans, drained and rinsed
- 1 cup corn kernels, fresh or frozen
- 1/4 cup chia seeds
- 1/2 cup plant-based cheese, shredded
- 1/4 cup fresh cilantro, chopped
- 1/2 red bell pepper, diced
- 1/2 tsp ground cumin
- 1/4 tsp smoked paprika
- Salt and pepper to taste
- Olive oil spray for cooking

Prep Time: 20 min   Cook Time: 10 minutes   Serves: 4

DIRECTIONS

In a mixing bowl, combine black beans, corn, chia seeds, cilantro, red bell pepper, cumin, smoked paprika, salt, and pepper. Mix well until all ingredients are well incorporated. Lay out 4 tortillas and evenly distribute the bean and chia mixture onto each one. Sprinkle with plant-based cheese, then top with the remaining tortillas. Preheat the air fryer to 350°F (175°C). Lightly spray the fryer basket with olive oil. Place quesadillas in the basket one at a time, ensuring they have space and don't overlap. Spray the tops lightly with olive oil. Air fry for about 10 minutes or until golden brown and crispy, flipping halfway through. Once cooked, let cool slightly, then slice and serve with your favorite salsa or guacamole.

NUTRITIONAL INFORMATION

Per serving: 310 calories, 12g protein, 55g carbohydrates, 6g fat, 11g fiber, 0mg cholesterol, 480mg sodium, 520mg potassium.

Toasted Almond & Lentil Bites

INGREDIENTS

- 1 cup cooked green lentils
- 1/2 cup toasted almonds, finely chopped
- 1/4 cup breadcrumbs (plant-based)
- 2 tbsp fresh parsley, finely chopped
- 1 garlic clove, minced
- 2 tbsp olive oil
- 1 tsp lemon zest
- Salt and pepper to taste
- Olive oil spray for cooking

 Prep Time: 15 min

Cook Time: 20 minutes

 Serves: 4

DIRECTIONS

In a large bowl, combine cooked lentils, toasted almonds, breadcrumbs, parsley, garlic, olive oil, and lemon zest. Mix well until all ingredients are well incorporated. Season the mixture with salt and pepper, then form into small bite-sized balls. Preheat the air fryer to 375°F (190°C). Lightly spray the fryer basket with olive oil. Place the lentil bites in the basket ensuring they have space and don't overlap. Spray the tops lightly with olive oil. Air fry for 20 minutes or until golden brown and crispy, shaking the basket occasionally to ensure even cooking. Once cooked, remove from the fryer and serve hot with a dipping sauce of your choice.

NUTRITIONAL INFORMATION

Per serving: 210 calories, 9g protein, 20g carbohydrates, 11g fat, 6g fiber, 0mg cholesterol, 80mg sodium, 320mg potassium.

Sesame Ginger Edamame Pods

INGREDIENTS

- 2 cups frozen edamame pods
- 2 tbsp sesame oil
- 1 tbsp freshly grated ginger
- 2 garlic cloves, minced
- 1 tbsp low-sodium soy sauce or tamari (for gluten-free)
- 1 tsp toasted sesame seeds
- 2 green onions, thinly sliced
- Red pepper flakes (optional for heat)
- Salt to taste

 Prep Time: 10 min

 Cook Time: 12 minutes

 Serves: 4

DIRECTIONS

In a mixing bowl, combine sesame oil, grated ginger, minced garlic, soy sauce or tamari, and a pinch of salt. Mix well. Add the frozen edamame pods to the bowl and toss them until they are well-coated with the mixture. Preheat the air fryer to 375°F (190°C). Transfer the coated edamame pods into the air fryer basket in a single layer. Cook for 12 minutes, shaking the basket halfway through. Edamame should be hot and slightly crisped on the outside. Transfer to a serving bowl, sprinkle with toasted sesame seeds, green onions, and red pepper flakes if desired. Serve immediately.

NUTRITIONAL INFORMATION

Per serving: 150 calories, 8g protein, 9g carbohydrates, 9g fat, 4g fiber, 0mg cholesterol, 200mg sodium, 500mg potassium.

Mighty Mushrooms

Garlic Butter Portobello Steaks

INGREDIENTS

- 4 large portobello mushrooms, stems removed and cleaned
- 4 tbsp vegan butter, melted
- 3 garlic cloves, minced
- 1 tbsp fresh thyme leaves
- 1 tbsp fresh rosemary, finely chopped
- 1 tbsp olive oil
- Salt and pepper to taste
- 1 tbsp lemon juice
- Fresh parsley, for garnish

Prep Time: 10 min

Cook Time: 15 minutes

Serves: 4

DIRECTIONS

In a bowl, combine melted vegan butter, minced garlic, thyme, rosemary, olive oil, lemon juice, salt, and pepper. Mix well. Brush each portobello mushroom cap generously with the garlic butter mixture, ensuring to cover all sides. Preheat the air fryer to 375°F (190°C). Once heated, place the portobello mushrooms in the fryer basket, gill side up. Cook for 12-15 minutes or until tender and slightly crispy. Once cooked, remove from the fryer, garnish with fresh parsley, and serve immediately.

NUTRITIONAL INFORMATION

Per serving: 170 calories, 3g protein, 9g carbohydrates, 14g fat, 3g fiber, 0mg cholesterol, 120mg sodium, 450mg potassium.

Shiitake Bacon Bits

INGREDIENTS

- 200g fresh shiitake mushrooms, stems removed and thinly sliced
- 2 tbsp olive oil
- 1 tbsp tamari or soy sauce
- 1 tsp smoked paprika
- 1/2 tsp garlic powder
- 1/2 tsp black pepper
- Pinch of sea salt

Prep Time: 10 min

Cook Time: 12 minutes

Serves: 4

DIRECTIONS

In a mixing bowl, combine sliced shiitake mushrooms with olive oil, tamari, smoked paprika, garlic powder, black pepper, and sea salt. Toss until the mushrooms are well coated with the mixture. Preheat the air fryer to 360°F (180°C). Once heated, evenly spread the coated shiitake slices in the fryer basket, ensuring they don't overlap. Cook for 10-12 minutes or until the mushrooms turn crispy, stirring once or twice to ensure even cooking. Remove from the air fryer, let cool for a few minutes to crisp up further, and use as a plant-based bacon bit substitute on salads, baked potatoes, and more.

NUTRITIONAL INFORMATION

Per serving: 80 calories, 2g protein, 6g carbohydrates, 6g fat, 2g fiber, 0mg cholesterol, 300mg sodium, 250mg potassium.

Balsamic Glazed Oyster Mushroom Skewers

INGREDIENTS

- 300g oyster mushrooms, cleaned and larger ones halved
- 1/4 cup balsamic vinegar
- 2 tbsp olive oil
- 2 garlic cloves, minced
- 1 tsp dried rosemary or thyme
- Salt and pepper to taste
- Wooden skewers, soaked in water for 30 minutes

 Prep Time: 15 min

 Cook Time: 12 minutes

 Serves: 4

DIRECTIONS

In a bowl, whisk together balsamic vinegar, olive oil, minced garlic, rosemary or thyme, salt, and pepper. Add the oyster mushrooms and marinate for at least 10 minutes. Preheat the air fryer to 375°F (190°C). Thread the marinated mushrooms onto the soaked wooden skewers. Place the skewers in the air fryer and cook for 10-12 minutes, turning halfway, or until the mushrooms are tender and have a nice glaze. Serve immediately, drizzled with any remaining marinade if desired.

NUTRITIONAL INFORMATION

Per serving: 100 calories, 3g protein, 9g carbohydrates, 6g fat, 2g fiber, 0mg cholesterol, 10mg sodium, 350mg potassium.

Crispy Maitake Tenders with Herb Dip

INGREDIENTS

For the Maitake Tenders:

- 300g Maitake mushrooms (also known as Hen of the Woods), cleaned and separated into tenders
- 1 cup almond milk or other plant-based milk
- 1 cup breadcrumbs (use gluten-free if needed)
- 1 tsp smoked paprika

For the Herb Dip:

- 1 cup vegan mayo
- 2 tbsp fresh dill, finely chopped
- 2 tbsp fresh parsley, finely chopped
- 1 garlic clove, minced
- Juice of 1/2 lemon

 Prep Time: 20 min

 Cook Time: 15 minutes

 Serves: 4

DIRECTIONS

In a shallow bowl, mix the almond milk, smoked paprika, salt, and pepper. In another shallow dish, place the breadcrumbs. Dip each Maitake tender into the milk mixture, letting the excess drip off, then coat with breadcrumbs, pressing them to adhere. Preheat the air fryer to 375°F (190°C). Place the breaded tenders in the air fryer in a single layer, ensuring they don't overlap. Lightly spray with cooking spray if desired. Air-fry for 15 minutes, flipping halfway through, until golden brown and crispy. While tenders are cooking, mix all herb dip ingredients in a bowl. Serve the crispy tenders with the herb dip on the side.

NUTRITIONAL INFORMATION

Per serving: 320 calories, 7g protein, 30g carbohydrates, 20g fat, 4g fiber, 0mg cholesterol, 450mg sodium, 410mg potassium.

Enoki Mushroom Crunch Rolls

INGREDIENTS

- 200g Enoki mushrooms, root ends trimmed
- 1/2 cup chickpea flour, sparkling water
- 1 tsp garlic powder
- 1/2 tsp turmeric (for color)
- 1 cup panko breadcrumbs (use gluten-free if needed)

For dipping sauce (optional):

- 2 tbsp soy sauce or tamari
- 1 tbsp maple syrup or agave nectar, sesame oil, seeds
- 1 green onion, finely chopped

 Prep Time: 20 min

 Cook Time: 12 minutes

 Serves: 4

DIRECTIONS

Combine chickpea flour, sparkling water, garlic powder, turmeric, salt, and pepper to make a pancake batter. Place panko breadcrumbs in a shallow dish. Dip Enoki mushroom bundles in the batter, coat with breadcrumbs. Preheat air fryer to 375°F. Arrange coated bundles in a single layer, air-fry for 12 minutes until golden and crispy. Mix dipping sauce ingredients. Serve hot with the dipping sauce on the side.

NUTRITIONAL INFORMATION

Per serving: 220 calories, 8g protein, 32g carbohydrates, 5g fat, 3g fiber, 0mg cholesterol, 320mg sodium, 310mg potassium.

Stuffed Cremini Caps with Spinach & Pine Nuts

INGREDIENTS

- 16 large cremini mushrooms, stems removed and finely chopped (reserve caps)
- 2 tbsp olive oil
- 3 cloves garlic, minced
- 2 cups fresh spinach, chopped
- 1/4 cup pine nuts, toasted
- 1/4 cup nutritional yeast or vegan parmesan
- Salt and pepper to taste
- Fresh herbs for garnish (optional: parsley or basil)

 Prep Time: 15 min

 Cook Time: 15 minutes

 Serves: 4

DIRECTIONS

Preheat the air fryer to 375°F (190°C). In a skillet over medium heat, add the olive oil. Sauté the garlic and chopped mushroom stems until softened, about 3-4 minutes. Add the spinach to the skillet and cook until wilted. Stir in the pine nuts, nutritional yeast or vegan parmesan, salt, and pepper. Mix well and remove from heat. Stuff each mushroom cap with the spinach and pine nut mixture, pressing down gently to pack the filling. Arrange the stuffed mushrooms in the air fryer basket in a single layer. Cook for 15 minutes or until the mushroom caps are tender and the tops are slightly golden. Garnish with fresh herbs if desired.

NUTRITIONAL INFORMATION

Per serving: 185 calories, 7g protein, 10g carbohydrates, 14g fat, 3g fiber, 0mg cholesterol, 55mg sodium, 520mg potassium.

Air-Fried King Oyster Pull-Apart "Ribs"

INGREDIENTS

- 4 large king oyster mushrooms
- 1/4 cup soy sauce or tamari
- 2 tbsp maple syrup
- 1 tbsp apple cider vinegar
- 1 tsp smoked paprika
- 1 tsp garlic powder
- 1/2 tsp onion powder
- 1/4 tsp ground black pepper
- 1 tbsp olive oil

Prep Time: 10 min

Cook Time: 20 minutes

Serves: 4

DIRECTIONS

Slice the king oyster mushrooms lengthwise into 1/2 inch thick slabs. In a mixing bowl, whisk together the soy sauce or tamari, maple syrup, apple cider vinegar, smoked paprika, garlic powder, onion powder, and ground black pepper. Coat the mushroom slabs in the marinade, ensuring they are fully covered. Let them marinate for at least 10 minutes. Preheat the air fryer to 375°F (190°C). Lightly brush the mushroom slabs with olive oil. Place the marinated mushroom slabs in the air fryer in a single layer. Cook for 20 minutes, flipping halfway, or until they are caramelized and have a pull-apart, "rib-like" texture.

NUTRITIONAL INFORMATION

Per serving: 90 calories, 4g protein, 12g carbohydrates, 3g fat, 2g fiber, 0mg cholesterol, 850mg sodium, 400mg potassium.

Panko-Crusted Button Mushroom Bites

INGREDIENTS

- 1 lb button mushrooms, cleaned and stems removed
- 1 cup panko breadcrumbs
- 1/2 cup unsweetened plant-based milk (e.g., almond, soy, oat)
- 1/2 cup all-purpose flour
- 1 tsp garlic powder
- 1 tsp onion powder
- 1 tsp dried thyme
- 1/2 tsp smoked paprika
- Salt and pepper, to taste
- Cooking spray or olive oil for light brushing

Prep Time: 15 min

Cook Time: 15 minutes

Serves: 4

DIRECTIONS

In a shallow bowl, mix the panko breadcrumbs with garlic powder, onion powder, thyme, smoked paprika, salt, and pepper. Pour plant-based milk into a separate shallow bowl and place flour in another. Dip each mushroom first into the flour, ensuring it's lightly coated. Dip it next into the plant-based milk, letting the excess drip off, and then coat it thoroughly in the panko mixture. Preheat the air fryer to 375°F (190°C). Arrange the coated mushrooms in a single layer in the air fryer basket, ensuring they do not overlap. Lightly spray or brush with oil. Cook for 15 minutes, or until golden brown, shaking the basket or turning the mushroom bites halfway through.

NUTRITIONAL INFORMATION

Per serving: 160 calories, 6g protein, 28g carbohydrates, 2g fat, 3g fiber, 0mg cholesterol, 170mg sodium, 380mg potassium.

Herb & Garlic Marinated Chanterelles

INGREDIENTS

- 1 lb fresh chanterelle mushrooms, cleaned and trimmed
- 3 cloves garlic, minced
- 1/4 cup olive oil
- 2 tbsp fresh lemon juice
- 2 tbsp fresh parsley, finely chopped
- 1 tbsp fresh thyme, finely chopped
- Salt and pepper, to taste

Prep Time: 30 min

Cook Time: 10 minutes

Serves: 4

DIRECTIONS

In a mixing bowl, combine garlic, olive oil, lemon juice, parsley, thyme, salt, and pepper. Stir well to combine. Add the chanterelle mushrooms to the bowl, ensuring each piece is well coated with the marinade. Let them marinate for at least 20 minutes. Preheat the air fryer to 375°F (190°C). Arrange the marinated chanterelles in a single layer in the air fryer basket. Avoid overcrowding; cook in batches if necessary. Air-fry for about 10 minutes or until the mushrooms are golden and slightly crispy on the edges.

NUTRITIONAL INFORMATION

Per serving: 160 calories, 3g protein, 10g carbohydrates, 13g fat, 3g fiber, 0mg cholesterol, 10mg sodium, 420mg potassium.

Szechuan Style Wood Ear Salad

INGREDIENTS

- 2 cups dried wood ear mushrooms, rehydrated and thinly sliced
- 2 tbsp soy sauce
- 1 tbsp rice vinegar
- 1 tsp sesame oil
- 1 tsp Szechuan peppercorns, toasted and ground
- 1 red chili, finely chopped
- 2 cloves garlic, minced
- 2 green onions, thinly sliced
- 1 tsp fresh ginger, minced
- A pinch of sugar
- Fresh cilantro, for garnish
- Sesame seeds, for garnish

Prep Time: 20 min

Cook Time: 10 minutes

Serves: 4

DIRECTIONS

In a mixing bowl, combine soy sauce, rice vinegar, sesame oil, Szechuan peppercorns, red chili, garlic, ginger, and sugar. Whisk the ingredients until well combined. Add the rehydrated wood ear mushrooms to the bowl and toss to coat them with the dressing. Preheat the air fryer to 370°F (190°C). Transfer the marinated wood ear mushrooms to the air fryer basket in a single layer. Cook for about 10 minutes, stirring halfway, until they get a slightly crispy texture. Allow the mushrooms to cool slightly. Before serving, toss in the green onions and garnish with fresh cilantro and sesame seeds.

NUTRITIONAL INFORMATION

Per serving: 60 calories, 3g protein, 10g carbohydrates, 2g fat, 4g fiber, 0mg cholesterol, 480mg sodium, 310mg potassium.

Truffle & Thyme Morel Crisps

INGREDIENTS

- 2 cups fresh morel mushrooms, cleaned and sliced thinly
- 2 tbsp truffle oil
- 1 tbsp fresh thyme leaves, finely chopped
- Sea salt, to taste
- Freshly ground black pepper, to taste
- 1 tsp lemon zest (optional for added flavor)

Prep Time: 15 min

Cook Time: 10 minutes

Serves: 4 servings

DIRECTIONS

In a mixing bowl, gently toss the thinly sliced morel mushrooms with truffle oil, thyme leaves, lemon zest (if using), salt, and pepper until well coated. Preheat the air fryer to 375°F (190°C). Arrange the seasoned morel slices in a single layer in the air fryer basket, ensuring they don't overlap. Cook for about 10 minutes, or until the morels are crisp and golden brown, shaking the basket or stirring the morels halfway through. Once done, transfer to a serving plate and serve immediately for the best flavor and crispiness.

NUTRITIONAL INFORMATION

Per serving: 90 calories, 2g protein, 6g carbohydrates, 7g fat, 2g fiber, 0mg cholesterol, 55mg sodium, 310mg potassium.

Porcini & Polenta Bites

INGREDIENTS

- 1 cup dried porcini mushrooms, rehydrated in warm water and finely chopped
- 1 cup instant polenta
- 3 cups vegetable broth
- 1 tbsp olive oil
- 2 cloves garlic, minced
- 2 tbsp nutritional yeast (optional for a cheesy flavor)
- Salt and pepper, to taste
- Fresh parsley, finely chopped for garnish

Prep Time: 20 min

Cook Time: 15 minutes

Serves: 4

DIRECTIONS

Boil vegetable broth, whisk in polenta, stir until thickened. Add nutritional yeast if using. Spread on a tray to cool. Sauté garlic in olive oil, add rehydrated porcini mushrooms, cook for 5-7 minutes with salt and pepper. Cut cooled polenta into bite-sized pieces, place porcini mixture on each. Preheat air fryer to 375°F, cook polenta bites for 10-12 minutes until golden and crisp. Garnish with fresh parsley before serving.

NUTRITIONAL INFORMATION

Per serving: 170 calories, 4g protein, 28g carbohydrates, 4.5g fat, 3g fiber, 0mg cholesterol, 480mg sodium, 210mg potassium.

Teriyaki Lion's Mane Nuggets

INGREDIENTS

- 2 cups Lion's Mane mushrooms, pulled into nugget-sized pieces
- 1/4 cup soy sauce or tamari for gluten-free option
- 2 tbsp maple syrup
- 1 tbsp rice vinegar
- 1 tsp sesame oil
- 1 clove garlic, minced
- 1/2 tsp ginger, grated
- 1 tbsp cornstarch
- 1 tbsp water
- 1 tbsp sesame seeds (for garnish)
- 2 green onions, thinly sliced (for garnish)

 Prep Time: 15 min

 Cook Time: 12 minutes

 Serves: 4

DIRECTIONS

In a bowl, whisk together soy sauce, maple syrup, rice vinegar, sesame oil, garlic, and ginger. In a separate small bowl, make a slurry by mixing cornstarch and water until smooth. Combine this with the sauce mixture. Marinate the Lion's Mane mushroom pieces in the sauce for about 10 minutes. Preheat the air fryer to 375°F (190°C). Once marinated, place the Lion's Mane pieces in the air fryer basket, ensuring they aren't touching. Cook for 10-12 minutes, or until they're golden and crisp. After cooking, toss the nuggets in any remaining sauce to coat them, and then garnish with sesame seeds and green onions.

NUTRITIONAL INFORMATION

Per serving: 110 calories, 3g protein, 18g carbohydrates, 2.5g fat, 1g fiber, 0mg cholesterol, 820mg sodium, 220mg potassium.

Rosemary and Red Wine Glazed Mushrooms

INGREDIENTS

- 2 cups mixed mushrooms (like cremini, shiitake, or button), cleaned and halved
- 1/2 cup red wine
- 2 tbsp olive oil
- 2 cloves garlic, minced
- 1 tbsp fresh rosemary, finely chopped
- Salt and pepper, to taste

 Prep Time: 10 min

 Cook Time: 15 minutes

 Serves: 4 servings

DIRECTIONS

In a mixing bowl, combine the red wine, olive oil, minced garlic, chopped rosemary, salt, and pepper. Toss the mushrooms in this mixture, ensuring they are well-coated. Let them marinate for at least 5 minutes. Preheat the air fryer to 380°F (193°C). Once ready, place the marinated mushrooms in the air fryer basket in a single layer, ensuring they aren't crowded. Cook for about 12-15 minutes, shaking halfway through, until the mushrooms are tender and slightly crispy. Once done, transfer to a serving plate. Drizzle any leftover marinade over the top for extra flavor.

NUTRITIONAL INFORMATION

Per serving: 90 calories, 2g protein, 4g carbohydrates, 6g fat, 1g fiber, 0mg cholesterol, 10mg sodium, 300mg potassium.

Grains & Bites

Crispy Quinoa & Veggie Patties

INGREDIENTS

- 1 cup cooked quinoa (follow package directions)
- 1/2 cup finely diced bell peppers (red, green, or yellow)
- 1/4 cup finely chopped red onion
- 1/4 cup grated carrot
- 1/4 cup grated zucchini, water squeezed out
- 2 tbsp ground flaxseed mixed with 6 tbsp water (as a binder)
- 1/4 cup bread crumbs (preferably whole grain)

 Prep Time: 20 min

 Cook Time: 15 minutes

 Serves: 4

DIRECTIONS

In a large mixing bowl, combine the cooked quinoa, bell peppers, red onion, carrot, zucchini, flaxseed mixture, bread crumbs, smoked paprika, garlic powder, salt, pepper, and parsley. Mix thoroughly until the mixture comes together. Form the mixture into patties (about the size of a medium burger). Preheat the air fryer to 375°F (190°C). Lightly brush each patty with olive oil on both sides. Place the patties in the air fryer basket without overlapping. Cook for about 15 minutes, flipping halfway through, until they are crispy and golden brown.

NUTRITIONAL INFORMATION

Per serving: 170 calories, 6g protein, 25g carbohydrates, 5g fat, 4g fiber, 0mg cholesterol, 80mg sodium, 320mg potassium.

Air-Fried Herb Risotto Balls

INGREDIENTS

- 2 cups cooked and cooled risotto (preferably made with vegetable broth)
- 1/4 cup fresh parsley, finely chopped
- 2 tbsp fresh basil, finely chopped
- 2 tbsp fresh chives, finely chopped
- 1/2 cup vegan mozzarella-style cheese, diced into small cubes
- 1 cup bread crumbs (preferably whole grain)
- 1/2 cup almond milk or any plant-based milk

 Prep Time: 30 min

Cook Time: 20 minutes

 Serves: 4 servings

DIRECTIONS

In a mixing bowl, combine cooled risotto with parsley, basil, and chives. Season with salt and pepper and mix well. Take about 2 tablespoons of the risotto mixture and flatten it in your palm. Place a small cube of vegan cheese in the center and roll the risotto around it, forming a ball. Repeat with the remaining mixture. Dip each risotto ball into the almond milk, then coat it in bread crumbs, ensuring it's fully covered. Preheat the air fryer to 375°F (190°C). Lightly brush each risotto ball with olive oil. Place them in the air fryer basket without overlapping and cook for 20 minutes or until golden and crispy, turning halfway.

NUTRITIONAL INFORMATION

Per serving: 320 calories, 8g protein, 52g carbohydrates, 9g fat, 3g fiber, 0mg cholesterol, 220mg sodium, 140mg potassium.

Spiced Couscous Samosas

INGREDIENTS

- 1 cup cooked couscous
- 1 tbsp olive oil
- 1/2 cup finely chopped onions
- 1/2 cup finely chopped bell peppers (mixed colors)
- 1/4 cup green peas
- 2 tbsp raisins
- 1 tsp ground cumin
- 1 tsp ground coriander
- 1/2 tsp turmeric
- 1/4 tsp chili powder (adjust to preference)
- 8 vegan samosa wrappers or phyllo dough sheets
- 2 tbsp plant-based milk (for sealing)

 Prep Time: 25 min

 Cook Time: 15 minutes

 Serves: 4

DIRECTIONS

In a skillet over medium heat, sauté onions in olive oil until translucent. Add bell peppers and green peas, cooking until softened. Stir in the raisins, spices, and couscous. Adjust salt to taste. Let the mixture cool. Take a samosa wrapper and place about 2 tablespoons of the couscous mixture on one side. Fold the wrapper into a triangle, enclosing the filling. Use plant-based milk to seal the edges. Preheat the air fryer to 375°F (190°C). Place the samosas in the basket without overlapping. Air fry for 15 minutes or until golden and crispy.

NUTRITIONAL INFORMATION

Per serving: 290 calories, 7g protein, 52g carbohydrates, 6g fat, 4g fiber, 0mg cholesterol, 180mg sodium, 230mg potassium.

Mediterranean Bulgur Wheat Pockets

INGREDIENTS

- 1 cup cooked bulgur wheat
- 1/4 cup diced cucumber
- 1/4 cup diced tomatoes
- 1/4 cup diced red bell pepper
- 1/4 cup chopped Kalamata olives
- 1/4 cup chopped fresh parsley
- 2 tbsp chopped fresh mint
- 2 tbsp olive oil
- 1 tbsp lemon juice
- Salt and pepper to taste
- 4 vegan pocket pitas

 Prep Time: 20 min

 Cook Time: 10 minutes

 Serves: 4 servings

DIRECTIONS

In a mixing bowl, combine bulgur wheat, cucumber, tomatoes, bell pepper, olives, parsley, and mint. Drizzle with olive oil and lemon juice. Season with salt and pepper, mixing well until all ingredients are well-incorporated. Cut a small opening at the top of each pocket pita and gently fill with the bulgur mixture.

Preheat the air fryer to 350°F (175°C). Place the filled pockets in the basket without overlapping and air fry for 10 minutes, or until they are slightly crispy and golden. Serve warm, preferably with a side of vegan tzatziki or hummus.

NUTRITIONAL INFORMATION

Per serving: 265 calories, 6g protein, 45g carbohydrates, 8g fat, 8g fiber, 0mg cholesterol, 270mg sodium, 220mg potassium.

Barley & Vegetable Spring Rolls

INGREDIENTS

- 1 cup cooked barley
- 1/2 cup julienned carrots
- 1/2 cup thinly sliced bell peppers (red, yellow, or green)
- 1/2 cup shredded purple cabbage
- 1/4 cup thinly sliced green onions
- 2 tbsp chopped fresh cilantro
- 8 vegan spring roll wrappers
- 2 tbsp low-sodium soy sauce
- 1 tbsp sesame oil, rice vinegar, grated fresh ginger

  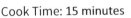

Prep Time: 30 min   Cook Time: 15 minutes   Serves: 4

DIRECTIONS

Combine cooked barley, carrots, bell peppers, cabbage, green onions, and cilantro in a bowl. Toss with soy sauce, sesame oil, rice vinegar, and ginger. Lay a spring roll wrapper flat, place 2 tablespoons of the mixture in the center, fold the bottom half, then sides, and roll tightly. Preheat air fryer to 370°F. Lightly spray spring rolls with cooking spray, place in the air fryer basket without touching. Air fry for 15 minutes until golden brown, flipping halfway. Serve with your favorite vegan dipping sauce like sweet chili or plum sauce.

NUTRITIONAL INFORMATION

Per serving: 210 calories, 5g protein, 40g carbohydrates, 3g fat, 5g fiber, 0mg cholesterol, 320mg sodium, 280mg potassium.

Farro & Mushroom Stuffed Peppers

INGREDIENTS

- 4 large bell peppers (any color), tops removed and seeds discarded
- 1 cup cooked farro
- 1 cup finely chopped mushrooms (like cremini or white button)
- 1 small red onion, finely diced
- 2 garlic cloves, minced
- 1/4 cup chopped fresh parsley
- 1 tbsp olive oil
- 1/2 tsp dried thyme
- 1/4 tsp red pepper flakes (optional)
- Salt and pepper to taste
- 1/4 cup vegetable broth

Prep Time: 20 min   Cook Time: 25 minutes   Serves: 4

DIRECTIONS

In a large skillet, heat olive oil over medium heat. Add the red onion and garlic, sautéing until translucent. Add the chopped mushrooms, thyme, and red pepper flakes, and continue to cook until the mushrooms have released their moisture and are golden brown. Remove from heat and stir in the cooked farro, fresh parsley, salt, and pepper, mixing until well combined. Carefully stuff each bell pepper with the farro and mushroom mixture, pressing down to compact the filling. Pour vegetable broth into the bottom of the air fryer basket to prevent the peppers from drying out. Place the stuffed peppers into the basket.

Set the air fryer to 375°F (190°C) and cook for 25 minutes or until the peppers are tender and the filling is heated through.

NUTRITIONAL INFORMATION

Per serving: 220 calories, 6g protein, 45g carbohydrates, 3g fat, 8g fiber, 0mg cholesterol, 150mg sodium, 600mg potassium.

Air-Fried Millet Tater Tots

INGREDIENTS

- 1 cup cooked millet
- 2 medium-sized russet potatoes, grated
- 1/4 cup finely chopped green onions
- 2 tbsp nutritional yeast
- 1/2 tsp garlic powder
- 1/2 tsp onion powder
- Salt and pepper to taste
- 1 tbsp flaxseed meal mixed with 2.5 tbsp water (flax egg)

 Prep Time: 15 min

 Cook Time: 20 minutes

 Serves: 4

DIRECTIONS

Make a flax egg by mixing flaxseed meal with water, letting it sit for 10 minutes until gel-like. In a large bowl, combine grated potatoes, cooked millet, green onions, nutritional yeast, garlic powder, onion powder, salt, and pepper. Add the flax egg, mix well. Shape into small cylinders or tots. Preheat air fryer to 375°F. Place tots in the basket in a single layer without touching. Cook for 20 minutes until golden and crispy, shaking the basket halfway for even cooking.

NUTRITIONAL INFORMATION

Per serving: 185 calories, 6g protein, 38g carbohydrates, 2g fat, 4g fiber, 0mg cholesterol, 10mg sodium, 400mg potassium.

Sweet Corn & Rice Fritters

INGREDIENTS

- 1 cup cooked rice (white or brown)
- 1 cup sweet corn kernels (fresh or frozen and thawed)
- 3 green onions, finely chopped
- 1/4 cup chickpea flour (besan)
- 1/4 cup fresh cilantro, finely chopped
- 1/2 tsp smoked paprika
- 1/2 tsp cumin powder
- Salt and pepper to taste
- 1 tbsp flaxseed meal mixed with 2.5 tbsp water (flax egg)

 Prep Time: 20 min

 Cook Time: 15 minutes

 Serves: 4 servings

DIRECTIONS

Begin by preparing the flax egg: Mix the flaxseed meal with water in a small bowl and allow it to sit for about 10 minutes until it forms a gel-like consistency.

In a large mixing bowl, combine the cooked rice, sweet corn kernels, green onions, chickpea flour, cilantro, smoked paprika, cumin powder, salt, and pepper. Add the flax egg and stir until the mixture binds together. Shape the mixture into small patties or fritter shapes, pressing them firmly so they hold. Preheat the air fryer to 375°F (190°C). Place the fritters in the fryer basket in a single layer, making sure they are not touching. Cook for 15 minutes or until they turn golden brown and crispy, flipping halfway through to ensure even cooking.

NUTRITIONAL INFORMATION

Per serving: 150 calories, 4g protein, 30g carbohydrates, 1.5g fat, 3g fiber, 0mg cholesterol, 25mg sodium, 250mg potassium.

Lemon Herb Freekeh Salad Bowls

INGREDIENTS

- 1 cup uncooked freekeh
- 2 cups vegetable broth or water
- 1 cup cherry tomatoes, halved
- 1 cucumber, diced
- 1/4 cup fresh parsley, chopped
- 1/4 cup fresh mint, chopped
- 2 tbsp olive oil
- Zest and juice of 1 lemon
- 1/4 cup red onion, finely chopped
- 1/4 cup Kalamata olives, pitted and sliced
- 2 tbsp capers (optional)

Prep Time: 15 min   Cook Time: 25 minutes   Serves: 4

DIRECTIONS

In a medium saucepan, bring the vegetable broth or water to a boil. Add the freekeh, reduce heat, cover, and simmer for 20-25 minutes or until the freekeh is tender and the liquid is absorbed. Allow it to cool. While the freekeh is cooking, prepare the vegetables and herbs. In a large mixing bowl, combine the cooled freekeh, cherry tomatoes, cucumber, parsley, mint, red onion, olives, and capers. In a separate bowl, whisk together the olive oil, lemon zest, lemon juice, salt, and pepper. Pour this dressing over the salad and toss to combine.

Serve the salad in individual bowls, either as a main or a side dish.

NUTRITIONAL INFORMATION

Per serving: 260 calories, 8g protein, 45g carbohydrates, 7g fat, 9g fiber, 0mg cholesterol, 280mg sodium, 310mg potassium.

Spicy Teff and Lentil Koftas

INGREDIENTS

- 1/2 cup teff grains
- 1 cup green lentils, rinsed and drained
- 2 cups water or vegetable broth
- 2 cloves garlic, minced
- 1 small red chili, deseeded and finely chopped (adjust to heat preference)
- 1/4 cup fresh cilantro, chopped
- 1/4 cup fresh mint, chopped
- 1 tsp ground cumin
- 1 tsp ground coriander
- Salt and pepper to taste
- 1 tbsp olive oil (for brushing)
- Lemon wedges, for serving

Prep Time: 20 minutes   Cook Time: 15 minutes   Serves: 4

DIRECTIONS

In a saucepan, boil lentils, teff, and water until tender and water is absorbed. Cool and transfer to a food processor. Add garlic, chili, cilantro, mint, cumin, coriander, salt, and pepper. Process until textured. Form into kofta shapes. Preheat air fryer to 375°F. Brush koftas with olive oil, place in the air fryer without touching. Cook for 12-15 minutes, turning halfway until golden and crispy. Serve hot with lemon wedges.

NUTRITIONAL INFORMATION

Per serving: 260 calories, 15g protein, 40g carbohydrates, 5g fat, 11g fiber, 0mg cholesterol, 220mg sodium, 320mg potassium.

Cumin and Lime Air-Fried Sorghum Bites

INGREDIENTS

- 1 cup sorghum grains, rinsed and soaked for 2 hours
- 2 cups water
- 1 tbsp olive oil
- 1 tsp ground cumin
- Zest and juice of 1 lime
- Salt and pepper to taste
- 2 tbsp fresh cilantro, finely chopped (for garnish)

 Prep Time: 10 min

 Cook Time: 20 minutes

 Serves: 4

DIRECTIONS

Drain the soaked sorghum grains. In a saucepan, combine sorghum and water. Bring to a boil, then reduce heat to low, cover, and simmer for about 45 minutes or until sorghum is tender. Drain any excess water and let it cool. In a mixing bowl, toss the cooked sorghum with olive oil, ground cumin, lime zest, lime juice, salt, and pepper. Ensure all grains are well coated. Preheat the air fryer to 375°F (190°C). In batches, spread the sorghum grains in a single layer in the air fryer basket. Air-fry for 20 minutes, shaking occasionally, until they are crispy and golden. Serve hot, garnished with fresh cilantro.

NUTRITIONAL INFORMATION

Per serving: 180 calories, 4g protein, 35g carbohydrates, 3.5g fat, 4g fiber, 0mg cholesterol, 150mg sodium, 180mg potassium.

Panko-Crusted Seitan Nuggets

INGREDIENTS

- 1 lb seitan, cut into bite-sized nuggets
- 1 cup panko breadcrumbs
- 1/2 cup unsweetened plant-based milk (e.g., almond, soy)
- 1 tbsp soy sauce or tamari
- 1 tsp garlic powder
- 1 tsp onion powder
- 1/2 tsp smoked paprika
- Salt and pepper to taste
- Olive oil spray (for cooking)

 Prep Time: 15 min

 Cook Time: 15 minutes

 Serves: 4

DIRECTIONS

In a mixing bowl, combine plant-based milk, soy sauce or tamari, garlic powder, onion powder, smoked paprika, salt, and pepper. Stir until well combined. Dip each seitan nugget into the wet mixture, ensuring it is well-coated. Then, roll each nugget in the panko breadcrumbs, pressing down gently to ensure the breadcrumbs adhere. Preheat the air fryer to 375°F (190°C). Lightly spray the nuggets with olive oil on all sides. Place the seitan nuggets in a single layer in the air fryer basket, ensuring they are not touching. Air-fry for 15 minutes, turning halfway, until golden brown and crispy. Serve hot with your favorite dipping sauce.

NUTRITIONAL INFORMATION

Per serving: 270 calories, 25g protein, 20g carbohydrates, 7g fat, 2g fiber, 0mg cholesterol, 480mg sodium, 220mg potassium.

Toasted Amaranth and Spinach Puffs

INGREDIENTS

- 1/2 cup amaranth grains
- 2 cups fresh spinach, finely chopped
- 1/4 cup nutritional yeast
- 2 tbsp ground flaxseed mixed with 6 tbsp water (flax egg)
- 1 tsp garlic powder
- Salt and pepper to taste
- 1 tbsp olive oil
- 1/4 cup water or unsweetened plant-based milk
- Olive oil spray (for cooking)

 Prep Time: 20 min

 Cook Time: 15 minutes

 Serves: 4

DIRECTIONS

Preheat the air fryer to 375°F (190°C). In a skillet over medium heat, toast the amaranth grains for 3-5 minutes or until they pop and become fragrant. Remove from heat and set aside. In a large bowl, combine toasted amaranth, chopped spinach, nutritional yeast, flax egg, garlic powder, salt, pepper, olive oil, and water or plant-based milk. Mix until everything is well combined and a thick dough forms. Shape the mixture into small balls and slightly flatten them into puff shapes. Lightly spray each puff with olive oil. Place the puffs in a single layer in the air fryer basket. Air-fry for 15 minutes, turning halfway, until they're golden brown and crispy on the outside. Serve immediately, preferably with a dip of your choice.

NUTRITIONAL INFORMATION

Per serving: 170 calories, 7g protein, 25g carbohydrates, 5g fat, 4g fiber, 0mg cholesterol, 75mg sodium, 300mg potassium.

Oats & Berry Breakfast Bites

INGREDIENTS

- 1 cup rolled oats
- 1/2 cup mixed berries (like blueberries, raspberries, and chopped strawberries)
- 1/4 cup almond butter
- 3 tbsp maple syrup
- 2 tbsp chia seeds
- 1 tsp vanilla extract
- Pinch of salt
- Olive oil spray (for cooking)

 Prep Time: 15 min

 Cook Time: 12 minutes

 Serves: 4

DIRECTIONS

Preheat the air fryer to 350°F (175°C). In a mixing bowl, combine rolled oats, mixed berries, almond butter, maple syrup, chia seeds, vanilla extract, and a pinch of salt. Stir until the mixture is well combined. Using your hands, shape the mixture into small bite-sized balls, pressing firmly so they hold together. Lightly spray each bite with olive oil and place them in a single layer in the air fryer basket, ensuring they don't touch. Air-fry for 12 minutes or until the bites are golden brown, turning halfway through cooking.

NUTRITIONAL INFORMATION

Per serving: 220 calories, 6g protein, 32g carbohydrates, 9g fat, 5g fiber, 0mg cholesterol, 40mg sodium, 180mg potassium.

Tofu &
Tempeh
Twists

Sweet Chili Tofu Bites

INGREDIENTS

- 14 oz (400g) firm tofu, pressed and cubed
- 1/2 cup sweet chili sauce
- 2 tbsp soy sauce
- 1 tbsp sesame oil
- 2 garlic cloves, minced
- 1 tbsp ginger, grated
- 2 tbsp cornstarch
- Olive oil spray (for cooking)
- Optional: sesame seeds and chopped green onions for garnish

 Prep Time: 20 min

 Cook Time: 15 minutes

 Serves: 4

DIRECTIONS

In a bowl, whisk together sweet chili sauce, soy sauce, sesame oil, minced garlic, and grated ginger. Add the tofu cubes, ensuring they're well coated. Let them marinate for at least 15 minutes. After marinating, gently toss the tofu cubes in cornstarch, ensuring they're lightly coated. Preheat the air fryer to 375°F (190°C). Lightly spray the tofu cubes with olive oil and place them in a single layer in the air fryer basket, making sure they aren't touching. Air-fry for 15 minutes or until the tofu bites are golden and crispy, turning halfway through the cooking process. Garnish with optional sesame seeds and chopped green onions before serving.

NUTRITIONAL INFORMATION

Per serving: 190 calories, 12g protein, 20g carbohydrates, 6g fat, 1g fiber, 0mg cholesterol, 700mg sodium, 250mg potassium.

BBQ Tempeh Ribs

INGREDIENTS

- 16 oz (450g) tempeh, sliced into "rib" strips
- 1 cup vegan BBQ sauce
- 2 tbsp soy sauce
- 2 tbsp apple cider vinegar
- 1 tbsp smoked paprika
- 1 tsp black pepper
- 1 tsp onion powder
- 1 tsp garlic powder
- Olive oil spray (for cooking)

 Prep Time: 25 min

 Cook Time: 20 minutes

 Serves: 4

DIRECTIONS

Whisk together BBQ sauce, soy sauce, apple cider vinegar, smoked paprika, black pepper, onion powder, and garlic powder in a bowl. Coat tempeh strips in the marinade and let them marinate for at least 20 minutes. Preheat air fryer to 375°F. Lightly spray tempeh with olive oil and arrange in a single layer in the air fryer basket. Air-fry for 20 minutes, flipping halfway, until the ribs are crispy and golden brown. Serve hot, drizzled with extra BBQ sauce if desired.

NUTRITIONAL INFORMATION

Per serving: 210 calories, 18g protein, 28g carbohydrates, 5g fat, 10g fiber, 0mg cholesterol, 680mg sodium, 450mg potassium

Crispy Tofu "Fish" Sticks with Vegan Tartar Sauce

INGREDIENTS

For the Tofu "Fish" Sticks:

- 14 oz (400g) extra-firm tofu, pressed and sliced into sticks
- 1 cup unsweetened plant-based milk (e.g., almond or soy)
- 1 tsp apple cider vinegar
- 1 tsp kelp or dulse granules (for the fishy flavor)
- 1 cup panko breadcrumbs
- 1 tbsp nutritional yeast
- 1 tsp garlic powder, onion powder, dried dill

For the Vegan Tartar Sauce:

- 1/2 cup vegan mayo
- 1 tbsp sweet relish, fresh lemon juice, dried dill

Prep Time: 30 min   Cook Time: 20 minutes   Serves: 4

DIRECTIONS

Mix plant-based milk, apple cider vinegar, and kelp or dulse granules. Place tofu sticks in the mixture and let marinate for at least 20 minutes. In another dish, combine panko breadcrumbs, nutritional yeast, garlic powder, onion powder, and dried dill. Remove tofu from marinade and coat each piece with the breadcrumb mixture, pressing the coating onto the tofu. Preheat the air fryer to 375°F (190°C). Spray the tofu sticks with olive oil and arrange in a single layer in the air fryer basket. Air-fry the tofu sticks for 20 minutes, flipping halfway through, until golden and crispy. While tofu is frying, mix together all tartar sauce ingredients in a small bowl. Serve tofu "fish" sticks hot with vegan tartar sauce.

NUTRITIONAL INFORMATION

Per serving: 260 calories, 12g protein, 24g carbohydrates, 12g fat, 4g fiber, 0mg cholesterol, 490mg sodium, 330mg potassium.

Teriyaki Tempeh Skewers

INGREDIENTS

- 1/2 cup low-sodium soy sauce or tamari
- 1/4 cup maple syrup or agave nectar
- 2 tbsp rice vinegar
- 2 garlic cloves, minced
- 1-inch piece of ginger, grated
- 1 tbsp cornstarch
- 8 oz (225g) tempeh, cut into cubes
- 1 red bell pepper, cut into chunks
- 1 green bell pepper, cut into chunks
- 1 onion, cut into chunks

Prep Time: 60 min   Cook Time: 15 minutes   Serves: 4

DIRECTIONS

Whisk together soy sauce, maple syrup, rice vinegar, garlic, and ginger. Set aside a few tablespoons and mix with cornstarch to make a slurry. Pour the slurry back into the sauce. Marinate tempeh cubes in the teriyaki mixture for at least 45 minutes. Preheat air fryer to 375°F. Thread tempeh cubes, bell peppers, and onions onto skewers. Lightly spray with olive oil. Place skewers in the air fryer basket, air-fry for 15 minutes, turning halfway, until tempeh is golden and vegetables are tender.

NUTRITIONAL INFORMATION

Per serving: 180 calories, 13g protein, 24g carbohydrates, 5g fat, 4g fiber, 0mg cholesterol, 850mg sodium, 350mg potassium.

Air-Fried Tofu Katsu with Curry Sauce

INGREDIENTS

- 14 oz (400g) firm tofu, drained and pressed
- 1/2 cup all-purpose flour
- 1 cup panko breadcrumbs
- 1/2 cup unsweetened plant milk (like almond or soy)
- 1 tsp apple cider vinegar
- 1 onion, finely chopped
- 2 garlic cloves, minced
- 1 carrot, finely chopped
- 2 tbsp curry powder
- 2 cups vegetable broth
- 2 tbsp soy sauce
- 1 tbsp agave nectar or maple syrup, cornstarch mixed with 2 tbsp cold water

Prep Time: 25 min

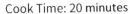

Cook Time: 20 minutes

Serves: 4

DIRECTIONS

Slice tofu into 1/2-inch rectangles. In one dish, mix plant milk and apple cider vinegar. In another, combine flour with salt and pepper. In a third, mix panko breadcrumbs with sesame seeds. Dip tofu in flour, then milk, and coat with breadcrumbs. Preheat air fryer to 375°F (190°C). Spray tofu with olive oil and air fry for 15-20 mins, flipping halfway. For curry sauce, sauté onion, garlic, and carrot. Add curry powder, vegetable broth, soy sauce, and agave. Simmer for 10 mins. Stir in cornstarch mixture until thickened. Serve with crispy tofu.

NUTRITIONAL INFORMATION

Per serving: 290 calories, 18g protein, 40g carbohydrates, 7g fat, 4g fiber, 0mg cholesterol, 780mg sodium, 410mg potassium.

Tempeh & Pineapple Tostadas

INGREDIENTS

- 8 small corn tortillas
- 8 oz (225g) tempeh, crumbled
- 1 cup fresh pineapple, diced
- 1 red bell pepper, diced
- 1/2 red onion, finely chopped
- 2 tbsp soy sauce or tamari
- 1 tbsp maple syrup
- 1 tsp smoked paprika
- 1 ripe avocado, diced
- 1/2 cup cherry tomatoes, halved
- 1 jalapeño, seeded and finely chopped
- Juice of 1 lime

Prep Time: 20 minutes

Cook Time: 15 minutes

Serves: 4

DIRECTIONS

In a bowl, combine crumbled tempeh, pineapple, bell pepper, and onion. Mix in soy sauce, maple syrup, and smoked paprika until everything is well-coated.

Preheat the air fryer to 375°F (190°C). Lightly spray both sides of the tortillas with olive oil. Place them in a single layer in the air fryer and cook for 4-5 minutes, or until crispy. In the same air fryer, place the tempeh and pineapple mixture in a single layer and cook for 10 minutes, or until lightly browned and heated through. While the tempeh mixture is cooking, prepare the avocado salsa by combining all its ingredients in a bowl. To assemble, place a generous spoonful of the tempeh and pineapple mixture on each crispy tortilla, and top with avocado salsa and cilantro.

NUTRITIONAL INFORMATION

Per serving: 310 calories, 15g protein, 35g carbohydrates, 14g fat, 8g fiber, 0mg cholesterol, 400mg sodium, 650mg potassium.

Tofu & Herb Stuffed Peppers

INGREDIENTS

- 4 large bell peppers (any color), tops removed and seeds discarded
- 14 oz (400g) firm tofu, crumbled
- 1 cup cooked quinoa
- 1/2 cup fresh parsley, finely chopped
- 1/2 cup fresh cilantro, finely chopped
- 2 green onions, thinly sliced
- 2 garlic cloves, minced
- 1 tbsp olive oil
- 1 tsp ground cumin
- 1 tsp smoked paprika
- Salt and pepper, to taste
- Olive oil spray (for cooking)

Prep Time: 15 min

Cook Time: 20 minutes

Serves: 4

DIRECTIONS

In a large mixing bowl, combine crumbled tofu, quinoa, parsley, cilantro, green onions, garlic, olive oil, cumin, smoked paprika, salt, and pepper. Mix thoroughly until well-combined. Stuff each bell pepper with the tofu and herb mixture, pressing down gently to ensure they are well-filled. Preheat the air fryer to 360°F (180°C). Place the stuffed peppers in the air fryer basket, making sure they stand upright. Lightly spray the outside of the peppers with olive oil. Cook for 20 minutes or until the peppers are tender and the filling is heated through. Serve immediately, optionally garnishing with extra herbs or a drizzle of olive oil.

NUTRITIONAL INFORMATION

Per serving: 210 calories, 13g protein, 25g carbohydrates, 7g fat, 6g fiber, 0mg cholesterol, 150mg sodium, 600mg potassium.

Spicy Black Pepper Tempeh Strips

INGREDIENTS

- 8 oz (225g) tempeh, sliced into thin strips
- 2 tbsp soy sauce or tamari
- 1 tbsp olive oil
- 1 tbsp freshly ground black pepper
- 1 tsp smoked paprika
- 1 tsp garlic powder
- 1/2 tsp cayenne pepper (adjust for desired heat)
- 1/2 tsp onion powder
- Olive oil spray (for cooking)

Prep Time: 10 min

Cook Time: 15 minutes

Serves: 4

DIRECTIONS

In a mixing bowl, whisk together the soy sauce, olive oil, black pepper, smoked paprika, garlic powder, cayenne pepper, and onion powder. Add tempeh strips to the marinade, ensuring each strip is well-coated. Let it marinate for at least 10 minutes. Preheat the air fryer to 375°F (190°C). Place the marinated tempeh strips in a single layer in the air fryer basket, ensuring they aren't overlapping.
Lightly spray the tempeh with olive oil. Cook for 15 minutes, flipping halfway through, or until the tempeh is crispy and golden brown. Serve immediately, perfect as an appetizer or added to salads, wraps, or stir-fries.

NUTRITIONAL INFORMATION

Per serving: 170 calories, 12g protein, 10g carbohydrates, 9g fat, 8g fiber, 0mg cholesterol, 520mg sodium, 300mg potassium.

Garlic & Lime Tofu Tacos

INGREDIENTS

- 14 oz (400g) firm tofu, pressed and cubed
- 3 tbsp soy sauce or tamari
- 2 tbsp olive oil
- 3 garlic cloves, minced
- Zest and juice of 1 lime
- 1 tsp chili powder
- 1 tsp cumin
- 1/2 tsp smoked paprika
- Olive oil spray (for cooking)
- 8 small corn tortillas
- Optional toppings: chopped cilantro, diced tomatoes, avocado slices, vegan sour cream

 Prep Time: 20 min
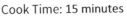 Cook Time: 15 minutes
 Serves: 4

DIRECTIONS

In a bowl, combine soy sauce, olive oil, minced garlic, lime zest, lime juice, chili powder, cumin, and smoked paprika. Add the tofu cubes and let them marinate for at least 15 minutes. Preheat the air fryer to 375°F (190°C). Place marinated tofu cubes in the air fryer basket in a single layer and spray lightly with olive oil.

Air fry for 15 minutes, shaking or flipping the tofu halfway, until crispy and golden brown. Serve the tofu on corn tortillas with desired toppings.

NUTRITIONAL INFORMATION

Per serving: 260 calories, 15g protein, 30g carbohydrates, 9g fat, 5g fiber, 0mg cholesterol, 480mg sodium, 350mg potassium.

Tempeh & Mushroom Dumplings

INGREDIENTS

- 8 oz (227g) tempeh, crumbled
- 1 cup mushrooms, finely chopped
- 3 green onions, finely sliced
- 2 garlic cloves, minced
- 1 tbsp soy sauce or tamari
- 1 tbsp sesame oil
- 1 tsp ginger, grated
- 24 vegan dumpling wrappers
- Olive oil spray (for cooking)
- Soy sauce, for dipping (optional)

 Prep Time: 25 min
 Cook Time: 15 minutes
 Serves: 4

DIRECTIONS

In a medium skillet, heat the sesame oil over medium heat. Add the garlic, ginger, tempeh, and mushrooms. Cook until the mushrooms release their moisture and the mixture is browned, about 5-7 minutes. Stir in the soy sauce and green onions, then remove from heat. Lay out the dumpling wrappers on a flat surface. Place a spoonful of the tempeh mixture in the center of each wrapper. Wet the edges of the wrapper and fold over, pressing to seal the edges. Preheat the air fryer to 375°F (190°C). Lightly spray the dumplings with olive oil and arrange them in the air fryer basket in a single layer. Air fry for 15 minutes, turning halfway, until the dumplings are golden and crispy. Serve with soy sauce for dipping, if desired.

NUTRITIONAL INFORMATION

Per serving: 290 calories, 18g protein, 40g carbohydrates, 7g fat, 4g fiber, 0mg cholesterol, 560mg sodium, 310mg potassium.

Sesame Crusted Tofu Steaks

INGREDIENTS

- 14 oz (400g) firm tofu, pressed and sliced into 1/2-inch thick steaks
- 1/4 cup soy sauce or tamari
- 2 tsp ginger, grated
- 2 garlic cloves, minced
- 1 tbsp maple syrup or agave nectar
- 3/4 cup mixed white and black sesame seeds
- Olive oil spray (for cooking)

 Prep Time: 15 min

 Cook Time: 20 minutes

 Serves: 4

DIRECTIONS

In a shallow dish, whisk together soy sauce, ginger, garlic, and maple syrup. Place the tofu steaks in the marinade, ensuring both sides are well-coated. Let marinate for 10 minutes. Remove tofu from the marinade and press each side into the sesame seeds, making sure the steaks are evenly coated. Preheat the air fryer to 375°F (190°C). Lightly spray the tofu steaks with olive oil and place them in the air fryer basket in a single layer. Air fry for 20 minutes, turning once halfway through, until the tofu is golden and the sesame seeds are toasted. Serve immediately with a side of veggies or rice.

NUTRITIONAL INFORMATION

Per serving: 210 calories, 16g protein, 10g carbohydrates, 13g fat, 4g fiber, 0mg cholesterol, 800mg sodium, 280mg potassium.

Buffalo Tofu Wings with Vegan Ranch

INGREDIENTS

- 14 oz (400g) firm tofu, pressed and cut into bite-sized cubes
- 1/2 cup buffalo sauce (ensure vegan)
- 2 tbsp cornstarch
- 1 cup vegan mayonnaise
- 1/4 cup unsweetened plant-based milk
- 1 tsp garlic powder, onion powder
- 2 tbsp fresh parsley, finely chopped
- 1 tbsp fresh dill, finely chopped
- 1 tsp apple cider vinegar

 Prep Time: 20 min

 Cook Time: 25 minutes

 Serves: 4

DIRECTIONS

In a large bowl, toss the tofu cubes in cornstarch until evenly coated. Preheat the air fryer to 375°F (190°C). Lightly spray the tofu cubes with olive oil and place them in the air fryer basket in a single layer. Air fry for 20 minutes or until golden and crispy, shaking the basket halfway through. In a separate bowl, toss the crispy tofu in buffalo sauce until well-coated. Return to the air fryer and cook for an additional 5 minutes. For the vegan ranch: In a mixing bowl, whisk together all the vegan ranch ingredients until smooth and creamy. Adjust salt and pepper to taste. Serve the buffalo tofu wings immediately with the vegan ranch dip on the side.

NUTRITIONAL INFORMATION

Per serving: 310 calories, 12g protein, 15g carbohydrates, 24g fat, 2g fiber, 0mg cholesterol, 890mg sodium, 290mg potassium.

Tempeh & Walnut Lettuce Wraps

INGREDIENTS

- 8 oz (227g) tempeh, crumbled
- 1 cup walnuts, finely chopped
- 2 tbsp soy sauce or tamari (for gluten-free)
- 1 tbsp sesame oil
- 1 tbsp maple syrup or agave nectar
- 1/2 tsp ginger powder
- 1/2 tsp garlic powder
- 1/4 tsp red pepper flakes (optional)
- 1/4 cup green onions, sliced
- 8 large lettuce leaves (e.g., iceberg, romaine, or butter lettuce)

Prep Time: 15 min

Cook Time: 20 minutes

Serves: 4

DIRECTIONS

In a bowl, mix crumbled tempeh, chopped walnuts, soy sauce, sesame oil, maple syrup, ginger powder, garlic powder, and red pepper flakes until well combined. Preheat the air fryer to 375°F (190°C). Transfer the tempeh-walnut mixture to an air fryer-friendly dish, spread evenly, and lightly spray with olive oil. Place the dish into the air fryer and cook for 15-20 minutes, stirring occasionally until the mixture is golden brown. Once cooked, let the tempeh-walnut mixture cool slightly and then mix in the sliced green onions. Spoon the tempeh-walnut mixture into lettuce leaves, garnish with fresh cilantro if desired, and serve with lime wedges on the side.

NUTRITIONAL INFORMATION

Per serving: 280 calories, 19g protein, 12g carbohydrates, 20g fat, 4g fiber, 0mg cholesterol, 460mg sodium, 400mg potassium.

BBQ Tofu Pizza Bites

INGREDIENTS

- 8 oz (227g) firm tofu, drained and cubed
- 1/4 cup BBQ sauce (vegan-friendly)
- 1/2 cup vegan shredded mozzarella cheese
- 1/4 cup diced red bell pepper
- 1/4 cup sliced black olives
- 1/4 cup thinly sliced red onion
- 1/4 cup diced pineapple (optional)
- 8 mini vegan pizza crusts or pita bread rounds
- Fresh basil or cilantro for garnish (optional)

Prep Time: 10 min

Cook Time: 15 minutes

Serves: 4

DIRECTIONS

Coat tofu cubes in BBQ sauce, marinate for 5 minutes. Preheat air fryer to 375°F (190°C). Air fry tofu for 10 mins until slightly crispy. Meanwhile, spread BBQ sauce on mini pizza crusts, top with vegan mozzarella. Once tofu is done, place cubes on pizzas, add bell pepper, olives, red onion, and pineapple. Air fry for 5 more minutes until cheese melts and edges crisp. Garnish with basil or cilantro, serve immediately.

NUTRITIONAL INFORMATION

Per serving: 280 calories, 12g protein, 35g carbohydrates, 10g fat, 4g fiber, 0mg cholesterol, 620mg sodium, 290mg potassium.

Breads &
Crusts

Mediterranean Stuffed Pita Pockets

INGREDIENTS

- 4 whole grain pita pockets
- 8 oz (227g) firm tofu, drained and crumbled
- 1 tbsp olive oil
- 1 tsp smoked paprika
- 1/2 tsp cumin
- 1 cup diced cucumber
- 1 cup diced tomatoes
- 1/2 cup thinly sliced red onion
- 1/4 cup chopped Kalamata olives
- 1/4 cup chopped fresh parsley
- 1/2 cup vegan tzatziki sauce
- 1/4 cup hummus

 Prep Time: 15 min

 Cook Time: 10 minutes

 Serves: 4

DIRECTIONS

Mix crumbled tofu with olive oil, smoked paprika, cumin, salt, and pepper in a bowl. Preheat air fryer to 375°F (190°C). Place seasoned tofu in a single layer in the air fryer basket. Air fry for 10 minutes until golden brown and slightly crispy.

While tofu cooks, combine cucumber, tomatoes, red onion, olives, and parsley in a bowl. Let the tofu cool for a minute. Assemble by spreading a tablespoon of hummus inside each pita pocket, add tofu and vegetable mixture, and drizzle with vegan tzatziki sauce. Serve immediately or refrigerate for up to 2 hours before serving.

NUTRITIONAL INFORMATION

Per serving: 320 calories, 15g protein, 45g carbohydrates, 9g fat, 7g fiber, 0mg cholesterol, 540mg sodium, 380mg potassium.

Rosemary Olive Focaccia

INGREDIENTS

- 1 3/4 cups all-purpose flour
- 1 tsp active dry yeast
- 3/4 cup warm water (110°F or 45°C)
- 1 tbsp olive oil, plus more for drizzling
- 1 tsp salt
- 1 tbsp chopped fresh rosemary
- 1/3 cup pitted Kalamata olives, halved
- Coarse sea salt, for sprinkling

 Prep Time: 90 min

 Cook Time: 12 minutes

 Serves: 4

DIRECTIONS

Dissolve active dry yeast in warm water in a small bowl; let it sit for 5 minutes until frothy. In a large mixing bowl, combine flour and 1 tsp salt. Add yeast mixture and 1 tbsp olive oil, mix until a dough forms. Knead the dough on a floured surface for 5 minutes until smooth. Place it back in the bowl, cover, and let it rise for 1 hour or until doubled in size. Preheat air fryer to 375°F (190°C).

On a floured surface, roll out the dough into a rectangle to fit the air fryer basket. Transfer to the basket. Press halved olives into the dough, sprinkle with rosemary and coarse sea salt, and drizzle with additional olive oil. Air fry for 12 minutes or until golden brown and cooked through.

NUTRITIONAL INFORMATION

Per serving: 270 calories, 7g protein, 50g carbohydrates, 5g fat, 2g fiber, 0mg cholesterol, 590mg sodium, 90mg potassium.

Air-Fried Vegan Calzones

INGREDIENTS

- 1 3/4 cups all-purpose flour
- 1 tsp active dry yeast
- 3/4 cup warm water (110°F or 45°C)
- 1/2 cup vegan marinara sauce, vegan mozzarella cheese, shredded, bell peppers, diced
- 1/4 cup black olives, sliced
- 1/4 cup red onions, finely chopped
- 1/2 tsp dried oregano, basil

Prep Time: 7 min

Cook Time: 15 minutes

Serves: 4

5

DIRECTIONS

Dissolve yeast in warm water; let sit for 5 mins. Mix flour, salt, yeast mixture, and olive oil. Knead, then let rise for an hour. Divide dough into 4, roll into circles. Spread marinara, vegan cheese, veggies, herbs on one half, fold, and seal. Preheat air fryer to 360°F (180°C). Cook calzones for 15 mins until golden brown, then cool before serving.

NUTRITIONAL INFORMATION

Per serving: 310 calories, 9g protein, 58g carbohydrates, 6g fat, 4g fiber, 0mg cholesterol, 620mg sodium, 180mg potassium.

Grilled Mackerel with Herb Salad

INGREDIENTS

- 4 mackerel fillets
- 2 tablespoons olive oil
- 1 lemon, zested and juiced
- Salt and pepper to taste

For the Herb Salad:

- 2 cups mixed fresh herbs (parsley, cilantro, dill)
- 1/2 red onion, thinly sliced
- 1 tablespoon olive oil
- 1 tablespoon apple cider vinegar
- Salt and pepper to taste

Prep Time: 15 minutes

Cook Time: 10 minutes

Serves: 4

DIRECTIONS

Combine warm water, sugar, and active dry yeast in a small bowl; let it sit for 5 minutes until frothy. In a larger bowl, mix flour and salt, then add yeast mixture and 1 tbsp olive oil. Knead into a smooth dough. Place in a greased bowl, cover, and let it rise for 60 minutes. Divide into 8 portions, roll each into a stick shape. Mix melted vegan butter with minced garlic, dried herbs, and 1 tbsp olive oil. Brush over each breadstick. Preheat air fryer to 375°F. Place breadsticks in the basket without touching. Cook for 12 minutes or until golden brown. Serve warm with melted vegan butter or marinara sauce.

NUTRITIONAL INFORMATION

Per serving: 280 calories, 6g protein, 51g carbohydrates, 6g fat, 2g fiber, 0mg cholesterol, 590mg sodium, 75mg potassium.

Spicy Jalapeño Cornbread Muffins

INGREDIENTS

- 1 cup cornmeal
- 1 cup all-purpose flour
- 2 tbsp sugar
- 2 tsp baking powder
- 1/2 tsp salt
- 1 cup almond milk
- 1/4 cup vegetable oil or melted coconut oil
- 1 tbsp apple cider vinegar
- 2 jalapeños, finely chopped (seeds removed for less heat)
- 1/2 cup corn kernels (fresh or frozen)

Prep Time: 15 min

Cook Time: 12 minutes

Serves: 4

DIRECTIONS

In a large bowl, whisk together the cornmeal, flour, sugar, baking powder, and salt. In a separate bowl, combine almond milk, oil, and apple cider vinegar. Mix the wet ingredients into the dry ingredients until just combined. Fold in the jalapeños and corn kernels. Preheat the air fryer to 375°F (190°C). If you have silicone muffin cups, place them in the air fryer basket. If not, lightly grease the basket. Fill each muffin cup 3/4 full with the batter. Place them in the air fryer basket, ensuring they're not touching. Cook for 12 minutes or until a toothpick inserted comes out clean. Allow muffins to cool for a few minutes before serving. They are best enjoyed warm.

NUTRITIONAL INFORMATION

Per serving: 320 calories, 5g protein, 52g carbohydrates, 10g fat, 3g fiber, 0mg cholesterol, 420mg sodium, 200mg potassium.

Vegan Naan with Garlic Butter

INGREDIENTS

- 2 cups all-purpose flour
- 1 tsp sugar
- 3/4 tsp baking powder
- 1/2 tsp baking soda
- 1/4 tsp salt
- 1/2 cup almond milk (or other plant-based milk)
- 1/2 cup plain vegan yogurt (like coconut or soy-based)
- 2 tbsp olive oil

For the Garlic Butter:

- 3 tbsp vegan butter, melted
- 3 garlic cloves, minced
- 1 tbsp chopped fresh cilantro or parsley (optional)

Prep Time: 75 min

Cook Time: 6 minutes

Serves: 4

DIRECTIONS

In a large bowl, combine flour, sugar, baking powder, baking soda, and salt. In another bowl, mix almond milk, vegan yogurt, and olive oil. Gradually add to dry ingredients and knead into a soft dough, adjusting with more flour if needed. Cover and let it rest for 1 hour. Divide the dough into 8 parts and roll each into a ball. On a floured surface, roll each ball into a 1/8-inch thick oval. Preheat air fryer to 400°F (205°C). Place a rolled naan in the basket, cook for 3 minutes on each side or until puffed and slightly golden. For garlic butter, mix melted vegan butter and minced garlic. Brush onto the freshly cooked naan, sprinkle with cilantro or parsley if desired.

NUTRITIONAL INFORMATION

Per serving: 320 calories, 6g protein, 52g carbohydrates, 9g fat, 2g fiber, 0mg cholesterol, 410mg sodium, 120mg potassium.

Sundried Tomato & Basil Pinwheels

INGREDIENTS

- 1 vegan puff pastry sheet, thawed
- 1/2 cup vegan cream cheese
- 1/3 cup sundried tomatoes in oil, drained and chopped
- 1/4 cup fresh basil leaves, chopped
- 2 garlic cloves, minced
- Salt and pepper to taste
- 1 tbsp almond milk (for brushing)

 Prep Time: 20 min

 Cook Time: 8 minutes

 Serves: 4

DIRECTIONS

Lay the puff pastry sheet flat on a lightly floured surface. Evenly spread the vegan cream cheese over the surface. Sprinkle the minced garlic, chopped sundried tomatoes, and fresh basil over the cream cheese layer. Season with salt and pepper. Carefully roll the puff pastry into a log. Slice the log into 1-inch thick pinwheels. Preheat the air fryer to 375°F (190°C). Place the pinwheels in the air fryer basket without overcrowding and brush the tops with almond milk. Cook for 8 minutes or until golden and crispy.

NUTRITIONAL INFORMATION

Per serving: 310 calories, 5g protein, 34g carbohydrates, 18g fat, 2g fiber, 0mg cholesterol, 320mg sodium, 180mg potassium.

Stuffed Vegan Pretzel Bites

INGREDIENTS

- 1 cup warm water (about 110°F or 45°C)
- 2 teaspoons sugar
- 2 1/4 teaspoons active dry yeast
- 2 3/4 to 3 cups all-purpose flour
- 1 teaspoon salt
- 1/2 cup vegan cheese, cubed (e.g., vegan cheddar or mozzarella)
- 1/2 cup baking soda
- 4 cups water (for boiling)
- Coarse sea salt, for sprinkling
- 1 tablespoon vegan butter, melted

 Prep Time: 30 min

 Cook Time: 10 minutes

 Serves: 4

DIRECTIONS

In a bowl, combine warm water and sugar, stirring until dissolved. Add yeast and let it sit for 5-7 minutes until frothy. Gradually add in the flour and 1 teaspoon of salt, kneading until a dough forms. Divide the dough into small pieces and flatten each piece into a circle. Place a cube of vegan cheese in the center, then fold the dough around the cheese, sealing it completely. In a large pot, bring the 4 cups of water to a boil. Carefully add the baking soda. Boil each pretzel bite in the water for 30 seconds, then remove with a slotted spoon. Preheat the air fryer to 400°F (205°C). Place the pretzel bites in the air fryer basket, ensuring they are not touching. Brush each bite with melted vegan butter and sprinkle with coarse salt. Cook for 10 minutes or until golden brown.

NUTRITIONAL INFORMATION

Per serving: 320 calories, 8g protein, 62g carbohydrates, 4g fat, 2g fiber, 0mg cholesterol, 2600mg sodium, 75mg potassium.

Crispy Bruschetta with Tomato & Basil

INGREDIENTS

- 4 slices of rustic bread, cut 1-inch thick
- 2 tablespoons olive oil
- 1 large garlic clove, halved
- 2 large ripe tomatoes, diced
- 1/4 cup fresh basil leaves, finely chopped
- 1 teaspoon balsamic vinegar
- Salt and pepper, to taste
- 1 tablespoon nutritional yeast (optional for a cheesy flavor)

 Prep Time: 10 min

 Cook Time: 5 minutes

 Serves:4

DIRECTIONS

In a mixing bowl, combine the diced tomatoes, chopped basil, balsamic vinegar, salt, and pepper. Stir well and set aside for flavors to meld. Brush both sides of the bread slices with olive oil. Rub the halved garlic clove over one side of each bread slice. Preheat the air fryer to 390°F (200°C). Place the oiled bread slices in the air fryer basket in a single layer. Air fry for about 5 minutes, flipping halfway, or until the bread is crispy and golden brown. Once toasted, remove the bread from the air fryer and immediately sprinkle with nutritional yeast if desired. Top each slice with the tomato and basil mixture.

NUTRITIONAL INFORMATION

Per serving: 190 calories, 5g protein, 27g carbohydrates, 7g fat, 2g fiber, 0mg cholesterol, 250mg sodium, 220mg potassium.

Vegan Cheese & Spinach Stuffed Rolls

INGREDIENTS

- 4 vegan dinner rolls or small ciabatta rolls
- 1 cup vegan mozzarella cheese, shredded
- 1 cup fresh spinach, finely chopped
- 2 tablespoons vegan cream cheese
- 1 tablespoon olive oil
- 1 garlic clove, minced
- 1/4 teaspoon salt
- 1/4 teaspoon black pepper
- 1/4 teaspoon red pepper flakes (optional)

 Prep Time: 15 min

 Cook Time: 8 minutes

 Serves: 4

DIRECTIONS

In a mixing bowl, combine vegan mozzarella cheese, finely chopped spinach, vegan cream cheese, minced garlic, salt, black pepper, and red pepper flakes. Mix until well combined. Cut a deep "V" into the top of each roll and gently remove some of the inner bread to create a pocket. Stuff each roll with the cheese and spinach mixture, pressing down gently to ensure it's well-packed. Brush the outside of each roll with olive oil. Preheat the air fryer to 375°F (190°C). Place the stuffed rolls in the air fryer basket in a single layer, ensuring they do not touch. Air fry for about 8 minutes or until the rolls are golden brown and crispy.

NUTRITIONAL INFORMATION

Per serving: 280 calories, 8g protein, 35g carbohydrates, 12g fat, 3g fiber, 0mg cholesterol, 580mg sodium, 150mg potassium.

Caramelized Onion & Olive Flatbread

INGREDIENTS

- 1 large onion, thinly sliced
- 2 tablespoons olive oil, divided
- 1 teaspoon balsamic vinegar
- 1 vegan flatbread or naan
- 1/2 cup kalamata olives, pitted and sliced
- 1/4 cup fresh parsley, chopped
- 1 teaspoon dried oregano
- 1/4 teaspoon salt
- 1/4 teaspoon black pepper
- 1/4 cup vegan feta cheese, crumbled (optional)

 Prep Time: 15 min

 Cook Time: 15 minutes

Serves: 4

DIRECTIONS

In a skillet over medium heat, add 1 tablespoon of olive oil. Add sliced onions and sauté until they become soft and begin to caramelize, about 10 minutes. Drizzle with balsamic vinegar, stir, and cook for another 2-3 minutes. Remove from heat. Brush the vegan flatbread with the remaining olive oil, ensuring the entire surface is covered. Spread the caramelized onions evenly over the flatbread. Sprinkle with sliced olives, parsley, oregano, salt, and black pepper. Preheat the air fryer to 350°F (175°C). Place the prepared flatbread into the air fryer basket and cook for about 5-6 minutes or until it's crisp and golden. Remove from the air fryer, sprinkle with vegan feta if desired, slice, and serve.

NUTRITIONAL INFORMATION

Per serving: 240 calories, 5g protein, 30g carbohydrates, 12g fat, 3g fiber, 0mg cholesterol, 650mg sodium, 170mg potassium.

Air-Fried Bagel with Vegan Cream Cheese & Chives

INGREDIENTS

- 4 vegan bagels, sliced in half
- 1 cup vegan cream cheese
- 1/4 cup chives, finely chopped
- Olive oil spray (optional for added crispiness)
- Salt, to taste

 Prep Time: 5 minutes

 Cook Time: 10 minutes

 Serves: 4

DIRECTIONS

Preheat your air fryer to 360°F (180°C). Lightly spray the bagel halves with olive oil spray. This step is optional but helps achieve a crisper finish. Place bagel halves in the air fryer basket, ensuring they don't overlap. Cook for 5-7 minutes, or until they're golden brown and crispy. While bagels are cooling slightly, mix the vegan cream cheese with chopped chives in a small bowl. Spread a generous amount of the chive cream cheese mixture onto each bagel half and serve.

NUTRITIONAL INFORMATION

Per serving: 290 calories, 10g protein, 45g carbohydrates, 8g fat, 4g fiber, 0mg cholesterol, 450mg sodium, 80mg potassium.

Sweet Potato & Sage Dinner Rolls

INGREDIENTS

- 1 cup mashed sweet potato (about 1 medium-sized sweet potato)
- 2 1/4 teaspoons (1 packet) active dry yeast
- 1/2 cup warm water (110°F or 45°C)
- 3 cups all-purpose flour
- 2 tablespoons olive oil
- 2 tablespoons maple syrup
- 1 teaspoon salt
- 1/4 cup fresh sage, finely chopped
- Olive oil spray for finishing (optional)

 Prep Time: 90 min

 Cook Time: 12 minutes

Serves: 6

DIRECTIONS

In a small bowl, dissolve the yeast in warm water and allow it to sit for 5 minutes or until frothy. In a large mixing bowl, combine the mashed sweet potato, olive oil, maple syrup, salt, and chopped sage. Add the yeast mixture and mix until combined. Gradually add the flour to the sweet potato mixture, kneading until a soft dough forms. Cover and let it rise in a warm place for about 1 hour, or until doubled in size. Divide the dough into 12 equal portions and shape them into rolls. Place the rolls into the air fryer basket, ensuring they don't touch. Cook at 330°F (165°C) for 12 minutes or until golden brown. Optionally, spray or brush with a bit of olive oil for a shinier finish right out of the air fryer.

NUTRITIONAL INFORMATION

Per serving: 230 calories, 6g protein, 48g carbohydrates, 2.5g fat, 3g fiber, 0mg cholesterol, 390mg sodium, 150mg potassium.

Olive & Rosemary Sourdough Crisps

INGREDIENTS

- 4 slices of day-old sourdough bread
- 1/4 cup black olives, finely chopped
- 2 tablespoons fresh rosemary, finely chopped
- 3 tablespoons olive oil
- 1/2 teaspoon sea salt
- 1/4 teaspoon black pepper

 Prep Time: 10 min

 Cook Time: 15 minutes

 Serves: 4

DIRECTIONS

In a small bowl, mix the finely chopped olives, rosemary, olive oil, sea salt, and black pepper until well combined. Spread a thin layer of the olive and rosemary mixture onto each sourdough slice. Cut each prepared sourdough slice into quarters or smaller, depending on the desired size of your crisps. Place the sourdough pieces in the air fryer in a single layer, ensuring they don't overlap. Cook at 350°F (175°C) for 15 minutes, or until the edges are golden and crispy, checking halfway and flipping if necessary.

NUTRITIONAL INFORMATION

Per serving (without dressing): 150 calories, 4g protein, 20g carbohydrates, 7g fat, 2g fiber, 0mg cholesterol, 400mg sodium, 60mg potassium.

Dips & Drizzles

Creamy Cashew & Herb Dip

Prep Time: 10 min

Cook Time: 0 minutes

Serves: 4

INGREDIENTS

- 1 cup raw cashews, soaked for at least 4 hours or overnight
- 1/4 cup water
- 1 garlic clove
- 2 tablespoons fresh lemon juice
- 1/4 cup mixed fresh herbs (like parsley, chives, and dill), finely chopped
- Salt, to taste
- Freshly ground black pepper, to taste

DIRECTIONS

Drain and rinse the soaked cashews. In a blender or food processor, combine the cashews, water, garlic, and lemon juice. Blend until smooth and creamy, scraping down the sides as needed. Transfer the blended mixture to a bowl and fold in the finely chopped herbs. Season with salt and freshly ground black pepper to taste. Serve immediately with air-fried vegetables or store in the refrigerator for up to 3 days.

NUTRITIONAL INFORMATION

Per serving: 170 calories, 5g protein, 10g carbohydrates, 13g fat, 1g fiber, 0mg cholesterol, 150mg sodium, 190mg potassium.

Spicy Mango Salsa

Prep Time: 15 minutes

Cook Time: 0 minutes

Serves: 4

INGREDIENTS

- 2 ripe mangoes, peeled and diced
- 1 red chili pepper, finely chopped (deseed for less heat)
- 1/2 red onion, finely diced
- 1/4 cup fresh cilantro, chopped
- Juice of 1 lime
- Salt, to taste

DIRECTIONS

In a mixing bowl, combine diced mangoes, chopped red chili pepper, and red onion. Add the fresh cilantro and lime juice to the mixture. Toss all ingredients gently to mix them well. Season with salt as per taste and give it one final mix before serving. Best served chilled.

NUTRITIONAL INFORMATION

Per serving: 70 calories, 1g protein, 18g carbohydrates, 0.5g fat, 2g fiber, 0mg cholesterol, 150mg sodium, 270mg potassium.

Vegan Tzatziki with Dill & Cucumber

INGREDIENTS

- 1 cup vegan yogurt (unsweetened)
- 1 medium cucumber, finely grated and drained
- 2 cloves garlic, minced
- 1 tablespoon fresh dill, chopped
- 1 tablespoon lemon juice
- 1 tablespoon olive oil
- Salt and pepper, to taste

Prep Time: 15 minutes   Cook Time: 0 minutes   Serves: 4

DIRECTIONS

In a mixing bowl, combine the vegan yogurt, grated cucumber, and minced garlic. Add the fresh dill, lemon juice, and olive oil to the mixture. Mix well. Season with salt and pepper according to your taste preference. Cover and refrigerate for at least an hour to allow flavors to meld. Serve chilled.

NUTRITIONAL INFORMATION

Per serving: 70 calories, 2g protein, 5g carbohydrates, 5g fat, 1g fiber, 0mg cholesterol, 100mg sodium, 150mg potassium.

Roasted Red Pepper Hummus

INGREDIENTS

- 1 can (15 oz) chickpeas, drained and rinsed
- 2 medium red bell peppers
- 2 cloves garlic
- 3 tablespoons tahini
- 2 tablespoons lemon juice
- 2 tablespoons olive oil
- Salt and pepper, to taste
- A pinch of paprika (optional)

Prep Time: 10 min   Cook Time: 15 minutes   Serves: 4

DIRECTIONS

Preheat your air fryer to 390°F (200°C). Place the red bell peppers into the air fryer basket and cook for 10-15 minutes or until the skin is charred and blistered. Remove and let them cool. Once cooled, peel off the skin from the bell peppers and remove the seeds. In a food processor, combine the roasted red peppers, chickpeas, garlic, tahini, lemon juice, and olive oil. Blend until smooth. Season with salt, pepper, and a sprinkle of paprika if desired. Serve with fresh vegetables or pita chips.

NUTRITIONAL INFORMATION

Per serving: 220 calories, 7g protein, 25g carbohydrates, 12g fat, 6g fiber, 0mg cholesterol, 200mg sodium, 300mg potassium.

Sweet & Spicy BBQ Drizzle

INGREDIENTS

- 1 cup tomato sauce (unsweetened)
- 3 tablespoons agave nectar or maple syrup
- 2 tablespoons apple cider vinegar
- 1 tablespoon olive oil
- 1 teaspoon smoked paprika
- 1/2 teaspoon chili powder (adjust to taste)
- 1/2 teaspoon onion powder
- 1/2 teaspoon garlic powder
- Salt and pepper, to taste

Prep Time: 5 min   Cook Time: 15 minutes   Serves: 4

DIRECTIONS

Preheat your air fryer to 350°F (175°C). In a mixing bowl, combine all ingredients and whisk well until the mixture is smooth. Pour the mixture into an oven-safe dish suitable for the air fryer. Place the dish in the air fryer and cook for 15 minutes or until the sauce has thickened and the flavors have melded. Let it cool slightly before serving. Drizzle over your favorite plant-based dishes or use as a dipping sauce.

NUTRITIONAL INFORMATION

Per serving: 80 calories, 0.5g protein, 18g carbohydrates, 2g fat, 1g fiber, 0mg cholesterol, 250mg sodium, 250mg potassium.

Vegan Nacho Cheese Sauce

INGREDIENTS

- 1 cup raw cashews (soaked in hot water for 30 minutes, then drained)
- 1/2 cup nutritional yeast
- 1 cup almond milk (unsweetened)
- 1 roasted red bell pepper (skin removed, can be from a jar)
- 1 tsp turmeric powder
- 1/2 tsp smoked paprika
- 1 tsp garlic powder
- 1 tsp onion powder
- 1 tbsp lemon juice or apple cider vinegar
- Salt and cayenne pepper, to taste

Prep Time: 10 min   Cook Time: 20 minutes   Serves: 4

DIRECTIONS

Preheat the air fryer to 320°F (160°C). Blend all the ingredients together in a high-speed blender until smooth and creamy. Adjust seasoning if necessary. Pour the mixture into an oven-safe dish suitable for the air fryer. Place the dish inside the air fryer and let it cook for 20 minutes or until the sauce has thickened and heated through. Once done, carefully remove from the air fryer and serve immediately over nachos or as a dip for your favorite snacks.

NUTRITIONAL INFORMATION

Per serving: 190 calories, 8g protein, 12g carbohydrates, 12g fat, 3g fiber, 0mg cholesterol, 120mg sodium, 350mg potassium.

Lemon & Caper Aioli

INGREDIENTS

- 1 cup vegan mayo (store-bought or homemade)
- 2 tbsp fresh lemon juice
- 2 garlic cloves, minced
- 2 tbsp capers, finely chopped
- 1 tbsp lemon zest
- Salt and black pepper, to taste
- 1 tbsp fresh parsley, finely chopped (optional for garnish)

Prep Time: 10 minutes

Cook Time: 0 minutes

Serves: 4

DIRECTIONS

In a mixing bowl, combine vegan mayo, lemon juice, minced garlic, chopped capers, and lemon zest. Whisk the mixture until all ingredients are well combined. Season with salt and black pepper according to taste. Transfer the aioli to a serving bowl and if desired, garnish with chopped fresh parsley. Store in the refrigerator for at least 1 hour before serving to allow the flavors to meld. Serve chilled.

NUTRITIONAL INFORMATION

Per serving: 200 calories, 0g protein, 4g carbohydrates, 20g fat, 0g fiber, 0mg cholesterol, 250mg sodium, 30mg potassium.

Avocado & Lime Crema

INGREDIENTS

- 2 ripe avocados, pitted and scooped out
- 3 tbsp fresh lime juice
- 1 garlic clove, minced
- 1/2 cup unsweetened plant-based yogurt (like coconut or almond yogurt)
- Salt and black pepper, to taste
- 2 tbsp fresh cilantro, chopped (optional)
- 1-2 tbsp water (if needed to adjust consistency)

Prep Time: 10 min

Cook Time: 0 minutes

Serves: 4

DIRECTIONS

In a blender or food processor, combine avocados, lime juice, minced garlic, and plant-based yogurt. Blend until smooth and creamy. If the mixture is too thick, add water 1 tablespoon at a time until desired consistency is reached. Season with salt and black pepper according to taste. If using, fold in the chopped cilantro. Transfer the crema to a serving bowl and refrigerate for at least 1 hour before serving. The cooling will help intensify the flavors.

NUTRITIONAL INFORMATION

Per serving: 170 calories, 2g protein, 12g carbohydrates, 14g fat, 7g fiber, 0mg cholesterol, 10mg sodium, 500mg potassium.

Sun-Dried Tomato & Walnut Pesto

INGREDIENTS

- 1 cup sun-dried tomatoes (not in oil), soaked in hot water for 10 minutes
- 1/2 cup walnuts, toasted
- 2 garlic cloves
- 1/2 cup fresh basil leaves
- 1/4 cup nutritional yeast
- 1/4 cup extra virgin olive oil
- Salt and black pepper, to taste
- 2 tbsp lemon juice
- 1/4 cup water or as needed

Prep Time: 10 minutes   Cook Time: 0 minutes   Serves: 4

DIRECTIONS

Drain the sun-dried tomatoes after they have softened from soaking. In a food processor or blender, combine the sun-dried tomatoes, toasted walnuts, garlic cloves, basil, nutritional yeast, and lemon juice. While processing, gradually add the olive oil in a steady stream until the mixture becomes a smooth paste.

Season with salt and black pepper according to taste. If the pesto is too thick, add water a little at a time to achieve the desired consistency. Transfer to a jar or container and refrigerate. Use as a spread, dip, or sauce as desired.

NUTRITIONAL INFORMATION

Per serving (excluding optional toppings): 290 calories, 7g protein, 12g carbohydrates, 25g fat, 4g fiber, 0mg cholesterol, 120mg sodium, 400mg potassium.

Smoked Paprika & Almond Spread

INGREDIENTS

- 1 cup almonds, unsalted
- 2 tbsp extra virgin olive oil
- 1 tbsp smoked paprika
- 2 garlic cloves
- Juice of 1 lemon
- Salt to taste
- 1/4 cup water (or as needed to blend)
- A handful of fresh parsley, roughly chopped
- 1 tsp agave syrup or maple syrup

Prep Time: 10 min   Cook Time: 8 minutes   Serves: 4

DIRECTIONS

Preheat the air fryer to 350°F (175°C). Place the almonds in the air fryer basket and roast for 6-8 minutes or until lightly golden. Allow to cool for a few minutes. In a food processor, blend the toasted almonds until they form a coarse meal. Add the olive oil, smoked paprika, garlic cloves, lemon juice, salt, and agave or maple syrup. Blend until well combined. Slowly drizzle in the water a little at a time while blending until you achieve a spreadable consistency. Stir in the chopped parsley by hand, and adjust the seasoning if necessary.

NUTRITIONAL INFORMATION

Per serving: 220 calories, 6g protein, 10g carbohydrates, 19g fat, 4g fiber, 0mg cholesterol, 60mg sodium, 300mg potassium.

Golden Turmeric Tahini Dressing

INGREDIENTS

- 1/2 cup tahini
- 3 tbsp lemon juice
- 1-2 tbsp water (adjust for consistency)
- 1 tbsp olive oil
- 2 tsp ground turmeric
- 1 garlic clove, minced
- Salt to taste
- A pinch of black pepper
- 1 tsp agave syrup or maple syrup

Prep Time: 5 minutes

Cook Time: 0 minutes

Serves: 4

DIRECTIONS

In a mixing bowl, combine the tahini, lemon juice, olive oil, ground turmeric, garlic, and agave or maple syrup. Whisk the ingredients together. As the mixture thickens, slowly add in water until you achieve your desired consistency. Season with salt and a pinch of black pepper, and whisk again to combine thoroughly. Store in an airtight container in the refrigerator for up to a week. Before serving, give it a good stir as separation might occur.

NUTRITIONAL INFORMATION

Per serving: 210 calories, 6g protein, 8g carbohydrates, 18g fat, 2g fiber, 0mg cholesterol, 40mg sodium, 180mg potassium.

Garlic & Chive Vegan Sour Cream

INGREDIENTS

- 1 cup raw cashews, soaked for 4 hours and drained
- 1/2 cup unsweetened almond milk (or any plant-based milk)
- 2 tbsp lemon juice
- 1 tbsp apple cider vinegar
- 2 garlic cloves, minced
- 2 tbsp fresh chives, finely chopped
- Salt to taste

Prep Time: 10 min

Cook Time: 0 minutes

Serves: 4

DIRECTIONS

In a high-speed blender, combine the soaked and drained cashews, almond milk, lemon juice, and apple cider vinegar. Blend until smooth and creamy. Transfer to a mixing bowl and fold in the minced garlic and chives. Season with salt to taste, and mix well until all ingredients are fully combined. Refrigerate for at least 1 hour before serving to allow flavors to meld. It can be stored in an airtight container in the fridge for up to 5 days.

NUTRITIONAL INFORMATION

Per serving: 130 calories, 5g protein, 8g carbohydrates, 10g fat, 1g fiber, 0mg cholesterol, 20mg sodium, 190mg potassium.

Spicy Peanut Dipping Sauce

INGREDIENTS

- 1/2 cup smooth peanut butter (unsweetened)
- 2 tbsp soy sauce or tamari
- 1 tbsp lime juice
- 1 tbsp maple syrup or agave nectar
- 1-2 tsp chili flakes (adjust to desired spice level)
- 1 garlic clove, minced
- 2-3 tbsp water (to reach desired consistency)
- 1 tsp toasted sesame oil (optional for added flavor)

Prep Time: 10 minutes Cook Time: 0 minutes Serves: 4

DIRECTIONS

In a medium-sized mixing bowl, whisk together the peanut butter, soy sauce, lime juice, maple syrup, and minced garlic. Add chili flakes according to your spice preference and mix well. Slowly whisk in the water, one tablespoon at a time, until you reach your desired consistency. For an added depth of flavor, stir in the toasted sesame oil, if using.

NUTRITIONAL INFORMATION

Per serving: 210 calories, 8g protein, 12g carbohydrates, 16g fat, 2g fiber, 0mg cholesterol, 520mg sodium, 230mg potassium.

Balsamic & Fig Reduction

INGREDIENTS

- 1 cup balsamic vinegar
- 4 dried figs, finely chopped
- 1 tbsp maple syrup or agave nectar
- 1/2 tsp vanilla extract
- Pinch of salt

Prep Time: 5 minutes Cook Time: 20 minutes Serves: 4

DIRECTIONS

In a small saucepan, combine the balsamic vinegar, chopped figs, and maple syrup. Bring to a simmer over medium heat. Reduce the heat to low and let the mixture simmer gently for about 15-20 minutes or until it has thickened and is reduced by half. Remove from heat and stir in the vanilla extract and a pinch of salt. Allow the reduction to cool to room temperature. It will continue to thicken as it cools.

NUTRITIONAL INFORMATION

Per serving: 100 calories, 0.5g protein, 25g carbohydrates, 0.2g fat, 0.8g fiber, 0mg cholesterol, 10mg sodium, 150mg potassium.

Sweet
Finishes

Air-Fried Apple Pie Pockets

INGREDIENTS

- 2 large apples, peeled, cored, and finely diced
- 1/4 cup brown sugar
- 1 tsp cinnamon
- 1 tbsp lemon juice
- 1 cup vegan puff pastry or pie dough
- 1 tbsp plant-based milk (for brushing)
- Powdered sugar (optional, for dusting)

 Prep Time: 20 min

 Cook Time: 12 minutes

 Serves: 4

DIRECTIONS

In a mixing bowl, combine diced apples, brown sugar, cinnamon, and lemon juice. Mix well and set aside. Roll out the vegan puff pastry or pie dough and cut into 8 circles using a cookie cutter or a glass rim. Place about 2 tablespoons of the apple mixture in the center of half the circles. Place the other circles on top and press the edges to seal, crimping with a fork for a decorative edge.

Brush the top of each pocket with plant-based milk. Preheat the air fryer at 180°C (350°F) and cook the pockets for 12 minutes or until golden brown. Let them cool slightly and dust with powdered sugar if desired.

NUTRITIONAL INFORMATION

Per serving: 270 calories, 3g protein, 45g carbohydrates, 10g fat, 3g fiber, 0mg cholesterol, 150mg sodium, 100mg potassium.

Chocolate & Hazelnut Stuffed Beignets

INGREDIENTS

- 1 cup all-purpose flour
- 1 tsp baking powder
- 1/4 cup sugar
- 1/2 cup almond milk (or any other plant-based milk)
- 1 tbsp coconut oil, melted
- 1 tsp vanilla extract
- Pinch of salt
- 1/2 cup vegan chocolate & hazelnut spread
- Powdered sugar for dusting
- 2 tbsp hazelnuts, chopped (for garnish)

 Prep Time: 45 minutes

 Cook Time: 10 minutes

 Serves: 4

DIRECTIONS

In a mixing bowl, whisk together flour, baking powder, sugar, and salt. Add the almond milk, melted coconut oil, and vanilla extract, mixing until a soft dough forms. Roll the dough on a lightly floured surface to about 1/4-inch thickness. Cut into 8 circles using a cookie cutter or a glass rim. Spoon a tablespoon of the vegan chocolate & hazelnut spread in the center of half the circles. Place the other circles on top and press the edges to seal, crimping with a fork for a decorative edge. Preheat the air fryer at 180°C (350°F). Cook the beignets for 10 minutes or until puffed and golden. Once done, allow them to cool slightly, then dust with powdered sugar and sprinkle with chopped hazelnuts.

NUTRITIONAL INFORMATION

Per serving: 320 calories, 4g protein, 52g carbohydrates, 12g fat, 3g fiber, 0mg cholesterol, 180mg sodium, 120mg potassium.

Coconut & Lime Sorbet Cones

INGREDIENTS

- 2 cups full-fat coconut milk
- 3/4 cup sugar
- Zest and juice of 2 limes
- 1 tsp vanilla extract
- Pinch of salt
- 4 vegan ice cream cones
- Toasted coconut flakes for garnish (optional)

Prep Time: 180 min

Cook Time: 5 minutes

Serves: 4

DIRECTIONS

In a blender, combine the coconut milk, sugar, lime zest, lime juice, vanilla extract, and salt. Blend until smooth and sugar is fully dissolved. Pour the mixture into a shallow dish and freeze for about 3 hours or until firm, stirring every 30 minutes to break up ice crystals. Preheat the air fryer at 160°C (320°F). Place the vegan cones in the air fryer and cook for 5 minutes or until slightly golden. Allow them to cool. Once the sorbet is frozen and the cones are cooled, scoop the sorbet into the cones. Garnish with toasted coconut flakes if desired.

NUTRITIONAL INFORMATION

Per serving: 295 calories, 2g protein, 41g carbohydrates, 15g fat, 1g fiber, 0mg cholesterol, 55mg sodium, 120mg potassium.

Cinnamon Sugar Vegan Donuts

INGREDIENTS

- 1 cup all-purpose flour
- 1/2 cup sugar
- 1 1/2 tsp baking powder
- 1/4 tsp salt
- 1/2 tsp ground cinnamon
- 1/2 cup almond milk (or any plant-based milk)
- 2 tbsp coconut oil, melted
- 1 tsp vanilla extract

Cinnamon Sugar Topping:

- 1/4 cup sugar
- 1 tsp ground cinnamon
- 3 tbsp melted coconut oil (for brushing)

Prep Time:15 min

Cook Time: 8 minutes

Serves: 6

DIRECTIONS

In a mixing bowl, combine the flour, sugar, baking powder, salt, and cinnamon. In another bowl, whisk together almond milk, melted coconut oil, and vanilla extract. Pour the wet ingredients into the dry and mix until just combined. Preheat the air fryer to 180°C (350°F). Roll the dough into small balls and flatten slightly to form donut shapes. Place them in the air fryer basket ensuring they don't touch. Air fry for 8 minutes or until golden brown and cooked through. Brush each donut lightly with melted coconut oil and then dip into the cinnamon sugar mixture.

NUTRITIONAL INFORMATION

Per serving: 215 calories, 2g protein, 35g carbohydrates, 7g fat, 1g fiber, 0mg cholesterol, 180mg sodium, 35mg potassium.

Blueberry & Almond Crumble Tarts

INGREDIENTS

For the Tart Base:
- 1 cup almond flour
- 1/4 cup coconut oil, melted
- 2 tbsp maple syrup
- A pinch of salt

For the Filling:
- 2 cups fresh blueberries
- 2 tbsp sugar
- 1 tsp lemon zest
- 1 tbsp lemon juice

For the Crumble Topping:
- 1/2 cup rolled oats
- 1/4 cup almond flour
- 2 tbsp coconut oil
- 2 tbsp maple syrup
- 1/4 cup sliced almonds

 Prep Time: 20 min

 Cook Time: 15 minutes

Serves: 6

DIRECTIONS

Tart Base: In a bowl, mix almond flour, melted coconut oil, maple syrup, and salt until a dough forms. Divide the dough into 6 and press each portion into the base and sides of tart molds to form a crust. Filling: In another bowl, toss the blueberries with sugar, lemon zest, and lemon juice. Divide the blueberry mixture among the tart bases. Crumble Topping: Mix the oats, almond flour, coconut oil, maple syrup, and sliced almonds in a bowl. Sprinkle the crumble topping over the blueberries in each tart. Preheat the air fryer to 180°C (350°F). Place the tarts in the air fryer basket and cook for 15 minutes or until the crumble is golden and the blueberries are bubbly.

NUTRITIONAL INFORMATION

Per serving: 320 calories, 6g protein, 28g carbohydrates, 22g fat, 5g fiber, 0mg cholesterol, 40mg sodium, 180mg potassium.

Air-Fried Banana & Nutella Spring Rolls

INGREDIENTS

- 6 vegan spring roll wrappers
- 3 ripe bananas, halved
- 6 tbsp vegan chocolate hazelnut spread (like a vegan version of Nutella)
- 1 tbsp coconut oil, melted (for brushing)
- Powdered sugar for garnish (optional)

 Prep Time: 15 min

 Cook Time: 8 minutes

Serves: 6

DIRECTIONS

Lay out each spring roll wrapper on a flat surface. Spread 1 tablespoon of vegan chocolate hazelnut spread on each wrapper. Place half a banana on top of the spread on each wrapper. Fold the sides of the wrapper inwards, then roll tightly to enclose the banana and spread. Seal the end with a dab of water. Brush each spring roll lightly with melted coconut oil. Preheat the air fryer to 200°C (390°F). Place the spring rolls in the air fryer basket without overcrowding and cook for 8 minutes or until golden and crispy, turning halfway through cooking.

NUTRITIONAL INFORMATION

Per serving: 270 calories, 4g protein, 45g carbohydrates, 10g fat, 3g fiber, 0mg cholesterol, 150mg sodium, 320mg potassium.

Sticky Pecan & Date Bites

INGREDIENTS

- 1 cup medjool dates, pitted and chopped
- 1 cup pecans, roughly chopped
- 2 tbsp maple syrup
- 1 tsp vanilla extract
- Pinch of salt
- Desiccated coconut for coating (optional)

Prep Time: 10 minutes

Cook Time: 10 minutes

Serves: 4

DIRECTIONS

In a food processor, combine the dates, pecans, maple syrup, vanilla extract, and a pinch of salt. Process until the mixture is well combined and sticks together. Form the mixture into small balls, about the size of a walnut. If desired, roll each bite in desiccated coconut for added texture and flavor. Preheat the air fryer to 180°C (355°F). Place the sticky bites in the air fryer basket without overcrowding and cook for 10 minutes or until they become slightly crispy on the outside.

NUTRITIONAL INFORMATION

Per serving: 280 calories, 3g protein, 40g carbohydrates, 15g fat, 4g fiber, 0mg cholesterol, 25mg sodium, 450mg potassium.

Raspberry & Chocolate Chip Vegan Muffins

INGREDIENTS

- 1 1/2 cups all-purpose flour
- 1/2 cup sugar
- 2 tsp baking powder
- 1/4 tsp salt
- 1/2 cup almond milk (or any plant-based milk)
- 1/4 cup coconut oil, melted
- 1 tsp vanilla extract
- 1 cup fresh raspberries
- 1/2 cup vegan chocolate chips

Prep Time: 15 minutes

Cook Time: 15 minutes

Serves: 6

DIRECTIONS

In a large mixing bowl, whisk together the flour, sugar, baking powder, and salt.

In a separate bowl, combine almond milk, melted coconut oil, and vanilla extract. Pour the wet ingredients into the dry ingredients and mix until just combined. Gently fold in the raspberries and vegan chocolate chips. Preheat the air fryer to 180°C (355°F). Fill silicone muffin cups about 3/4 full with the batter and place them in the air fryer basket. Air fry for 15 minutes or until a toothpick inserted into the center comes out clean.

NUTRITIONAL INFORMATION

Per serving: 320 calories, 5g protein, 52g carbohydrates, 12g fat, 3g fiber, 0mg cholesterol, 200mg sodium, 125mg potassium.

Crispy Peach & Vanilla Turnovers

INGREDIENTS

- 2 fresh peaches, peeled and diced
- 1/4 cup brown sugar
- 1 tsp vanilla extract
- 1 tbsp cornstarch
- 2 tbsp water
- 1 package vegan puff pastry, thawed
- 1 tbsp almond milk (for brushing)
- Powdered sugar (for dusting, optional)

Prep Time: 20 min

Cook Time: 10 minutes

Serves: 6

DIRECTIONS

In a medium-sized saucepan, combine the diced peaches, brown sugar, and vanilla extract. Cook over medium heat until the peaches soften. In a small bowl, mix cornstarch with water to create a slurry. Pour into the peach mixture and stir until thickened. Remove from heat and let cool. Roll out the vegan puff pastry and cut into squares or circles. Spoon a portion of the peach mixture into the center of each pastry piece. Fold over to create a half-moon shape and crimp the edges using a fork. Preheat the air fryer to 200°C (390°F). Brush each turnover with almond milk. Place the turnovers in the air fryer basket ensuring they don't touch. Air fry for 10 minutes or until golden brown. If desired, dust with powdered sugar before serving.

NUTRITIONAL INFORMATION

Per serving: 275 calories, 4g protein, 40g carbohydrates, 12g fat, 2g fiber, 0mg cholesterol, 210mg sodium, 150mg potassium.

Air-Fried Churros with Vegan Chocolate Sauce

INGREDIENTS

- 1 cup water
- 2 tbsp vegan butter
- 1 cup all-purpose flour
- A pinch of salt
- 1 tsp vanilla extract
- 1/4 cup granulated sugar (for coating)
- 1 tsp cinnamon powder (for coating)
- 1/2 cup vegan dark chocolate chips
- 1/4 cup coconut milk (full fat)
- 1/2 tsp vanilla extract

Prep Time:15 min

Cook Time: 10 minutes

Serves: 6

DIRECTIONS

Boil water and vegan butter, add flour, salt, stir until a ball forms. Remove from heat, add vanilla, and cool. Pipe onto tray, cut, and air fry at 190°C for 10 mins.
Roll warm churros in sugar-cinnamon mix. For the sauce: Microwave vegan chocolate chips with coconut milk, stir in vanilla. Serve churros warm with chocolate sauce.

NUTRITIONAL INFORMATION

Per serving: 290 calories, 4g protein, 46g carbohydrates, 11g fat, 3g fiber, 0mg cholesterol, 55mg sodium, 90mg potassium.

Lemon & Poppy Seed Glazed Cookies

INGREDIENTS

- 1 cup all-purpose flour
- 1/2 cup granulated sugar
- 1/4 cup vegan butter, softened
- 1 tsp baking powder
- 1 tbsp poppy seeds
- Zest of 1 lemon
- 2 tbsp fresh lemon juice
- 1/4 cup unsweetened plant-based milk (like almond or soy)
- 1 cup powdered sugar
- 1-2 tbsp fresh lemon juice
- 1 tbsp poppy seeds for garnish

 Prep Time: 20 min

 Cook Time: 12 minutes

 Serves: 6

DIRECTIONS

In a mixing bowl, cream together vegan butter and sugar until light and fluffy. Stir in lemon zest, lemon juice, and plant-based milk. In a separate bowl, whisk together the flour, baking powder, and poppy seeds. Gradually add the dry mixture to the wet mixture, mixing until a soft dough forms. Form the dough into small balls and flatten slightly. Arrange them on a parchment-lined tray with space between each cookie. Preheat the air fryer to 180°C (350°F). Place cookies in the air fryer basket in a single layer, ensuring they don't touch. Air fry for 10-12 minutes or until lightly golden. For the glaze: Whisk together powdered sugar and lemon juice until smooth. Once cookies have cooled, drizzle with the glaze and sprinkle additional poppy seeds on top.

NUTRITIONAL INFORMATION

Per serving: 260 calories, 3g protein, 50g carbohydrates, 6g fat, 1g fiber, 0mg cholesterol, 110mg sodium, 50mg potassium.

Chocolate Avocado Brownie Bites

INGREDIENTS

- 1 ripe avocado, mashed
- 1/4 cup unsweetened cocoa powder
- 1/2 cup coconut sugar or maple syrup
- 1 tsp vanilla extract
- 2 tbsp flaxseed meal (mixed with 5 tbsp water, let sit for 5 minutes to make a flax egg)
- 1/2 cup all-purpose flour or oat flour for a gluten-free version
- 1/2 tsp baking soda
- 1/4 tsp salt
- 1/4 cup vegan chocolate chips

 Prep Time: 15 min

 Cook Time: 12 minutes

 Serves: 6

DIRECTIONS

In a mixing bowl, combine mashed avocado, cocoa powder, coconut sugar or maple syrup, and vanilla extract. Mix until smooth and well combined. Stir in the flax egg. Then, gradually mix in the flour, baking soda, and salt. Once combined, fold in the vegan chocolate chips. Form the mixture into small bite-sized balls and place them on a parchment-lined tray. Preheat the air fryer to 180°C (350°F). Place the brownie bites in the air fryer basket in a single layer, ensuring they don't touch. Air fry for 10-12 minutes or until firm to the touch. Allow brownie bites to cool before serving.

NUTRITIONAL INFORMATION

Per serving: 190 calories, 3g protein, 30g carbohydrates, 7g fat, 4g fiber, 0mg cholesterol, 140mg sodium, 250mg potassium.

Strawberry & Cream Cheese Pastry Twists

INGREDIENTS

- 1 sheet of vegan puff pastry, thawed
- 1/2 cup vegan cream cheese, softened
- 1/4 cup fresh strawberries, finely chopped
- 2 tbsp coconut sugar or powdered sugar
- 1 tsp vanilla extract
- 2 tbsp almond milk or other plant-based milk (for brushing)
- Optional: powdered sugar for dusting

 Prep Time: 20 min

 Cook Time: 12 minutes

 Serves: 4

DIRECTIONS

In a mixing bowl, combine the vegan cream cheese, chopped strawberries, sugar, and vanilla extract. Mix until smooth and well blended. Roll out the puff pastry on a lightly floured surface into a rectangle. Cut into 8 long strips. Spread a thin layer of the cream cheese mixture onto one side of each strip. Twist each strip several times, then lay them on a parchment-lined tray. Brush the tops of the pastry twists with almond milk. Preheat the air fryer to 190°C (375°F). Place the pastry twists in the air fryer basket in a single layer, ensuring they don't touch. Air fry for 10-12 minutes or until golden brown. Allow the pastry twists to cool slightly, then optionally dust with powdered sugar before serving.

NUTRITIONAL INFORMATION

Per serving: 270 calories, 4g protein, 30g carbohydrates, 15g fat, 2g fiber, 0mg cholesterol, 220mg sodium, 80mg potassium.

Vegan S'mores Pockets

INGREDIENTS

- 1 package vegan pie dough or puff pastry
- 1/2 cup vegan chocolate chips
- 1/2 cup vegan mini marshmallows
- 1/4 cup crushed vegan graham crackers
- 1 tbsp plant-based milk (for sealing and brushing)
- Optional: powdered sugar for dusting

 Prep Time:15 min

 Cook Time: 8 minutes

 Serves: 4

DIRECTIONS

Roll out vegan pie dough on a floured surface, cut into eight squares. On four squares, place vegan chocolate chips, mini marshmallows, and crushed graham crackers. Top with the remaining squares, crimp edges with a fork. Brush with plant-based milk. Preheat air fryer to 180°C (350°F). Place s'mores pockets in the basket, ensuring no overlap. Cook for 7-8 minutes until golden brown. Cool, optionally dust with powdered sugar before serving.

NUTRITIONAL INFORMATION

Per serving: 280 calories, 3g protein, 35g carbohydrates, 14g fat, 1g fiber, 0mg cholesterol, 170mg sodium, 70mg potassium.

Measurement Conversion Charts

MEASUREMENT

Cup	Ounces	Milliliters	Tablespoons
8 cups	64 oz	1895 ml	128
6 cups	48 oz	1420 ml	96
5 cups	40 oz	1180 ml	80
4 cups	32 oz	960 ml	64
2 cups	16 oz	480 ml	32
1 cup	8 oz	240 ml	16
3/4 cup	6 oz	177 ml	12
2/3 cup	5 oz	158 ml	11
1/2 cup	4 oz	118 ml	8
3/8 cup	3 oz	90 ml	6
1/3 cup	2.5 oz	79 ml	5.5
1/4 cup	2 oz	59 ml	4
1/8 cup	1 oz	30 ml	3
1/16 cup	1/2 oz	15 ml	1

WEIGHT

Imperial	Metric
1/2 oz	15 g
1 oz	29 g
2 oz	57 g
3 oz	85 g
4 oz	113 g
5 oz	141 g
6 oz	170 g
8 oz	227 g
10 oz	283 g
12 oz	340 g
13 oz	369 g
14 oz	397 g
15 oz	425 g
1 lb	453 g

TEMPERATURE

Fahrenheit	Celsius
100 °F	37 °C
150 °F	65 °C
200 °F	93 °C
250 °F	121 °C
300 °F	150 °C
325 °F	160 °C
350 °F	180 °C
375 °F	190 °C
400 °F	200 °C
425 °F	220 °C
450 °F	230 °C
500 °F	260 °C
525 °F	274 °C
550 °F	288 °C

Made in the USA
Las Vegas, NV
09 November 2024

11386826R00057

GREYSCALE

BIN TRAVELER FORM

Cut By _Marionjel_ Qty _30_ Date _07/30_

Scanned By _____ Qty_____ Date _____

Scanned Batch IDs

_____

Notes / Exception

_____

_____

_____

_____

_____